Business Partners

Pearson Brown
John Allison

Language Teaching Publications
35 Church Road Hove BN3 2BE

This book is fully protected by copyright.
All rights reserved. No part of this publication
may be reproduced, stored in a retrieval system,
or transmitted in any form or by any means,
electronic, mechanical, photocopying, recording,
or otherwise, without prior permission of the
copyright owner.

© Language Teaching Publications, Pearson Brown and John Allison, 1991

ISBN	Students' Book	0 906717 81 7
	Teachers' Manual	0 906717 84 1
	Workbook	0 906717 82 5
	Cassette	0 906717 83 3

The Authors

Pearson Brown and John Allison have specialised in the teaching of business English. They work in France at English International in Lyon.

Acknowledgements

We are grateful to the following for permission to reproduce extracts from books of which they are copyright holders:
Associated Book Publishers (U.K.) Ltd for So You Think You Can Sell by Video Arts; Columbus Books for The Extremely Serious Guide to Business by Keith Ray; Collins for What They Don't Teach You at Harvard Business School by Marc McCormack; Macdonald and Co. for Getting Things Done by Edwin C Bliss; Random House Inc. for Up the Organisation by Michael Greaves; Kogan Page for How to Be a Better Manager by Michael Armstrong; Transworld Publishers Ltd. for Iacocca: An Autobiography by Lee Iacocca with William Novak; Grafton Books a division of the Collins Publishing Group for the Official Guide to Success and How to Master the Art of Selling by Tom Hopkins; Collins for The One Minute Manager by Kenneth Branchard and Spencer Johnson. Punch for several cartoons.

Illustrations by Ian Andrew and Nigel Ellis.
Cover by Bridgewater Design Ltd.

Printed in England by Commercial Colour Press, London E7.

Contents

UNIT 1	CANTON COMPUTERS	6

Telephone language
Numbers
Business Vocabulary
Text: *So You Think You Can Sell*

UNIT 2	THE EXPENSE CLAIM	16

Past Simple
Questions and Negatives
Key Vocabulary
Text: *The Extremely Serious Guide to Business*

UNIT 3	STEPNIEWSKI	26

Polite Requests
Answering Requests
Eating out
Text: *What They Don't Teach You At Harvard Business School*

UNIT 4	YORK	36

Present Perfect
Adverbs of time
Vocabulary
Text: *The Extremely Serious Guide to Business*

UNIT 5	MANCHESTER	46

Present Simple
Present Continuous
Adverbs of frequency
Important words
Text: *Getting Things Done*

UNIT 6	THE TRADE FAIR	56

Present continuous for the future
(be) going to
Business Vocabulary
Text: *Up The Organisation*

UNIT 7	CASH FLOW	66

Predictions
Decisions
Offers and Promises
Future verb forms
Text: *How to be a Better Manager*

| UNIT 8 | FENTON | 76 |

Tags and closing questions
Vocabulary
Prepositions
Text: *Iacocca, an autobiography*

| UNIT 9 | SOPHIA ANTIPOLIS | 86 |

Checking and correcting information
Confirming with tags
Two-word expressions
Text: *The Official Guide to Success*

| UNIT 10 | COMMODITIES | 96 |

Describing graphs
Prepositions of time
Business Game

| UNIT 11 | HEADHUNTING | 104 |

First conditional
'When' plus 'will'
Vocabulary
Text: *The Official Guide to Success*

| UNIT 12 | FRINGE BENEFITS | 114 |

'Must' and 'have to'
Offers and suggestions
Financial Vocabulary
Text: *The One Minute Manager*

| UNIT 13 | WHITE WIDGETS | 124 |

Second conditional
First and Second conditionals
Vocabulary
Text: *The One Minute Manager*

| UNIT 14 | THE TRAINEE | 134 |

Giving Advice
Present simple and continuous
Vocabulary
Text: *How to Master the Art of Selling*

| UNIT 15 | A PRESENTATION | 144 |

All language needed for presentations

| LISTENING TEXTS | | 152 |

To the Student

Business Partners will help you with the language you need for work. That means both 'business English' and some of the language you need for social situations.

There are 15 Units. Each one has four important parts:

- **a dialogue** in the book and recorded on tape which gives you lots of useful language.

- **exercises** to help you with pronunciation, grammar and vocabulary.

- **a role play** where you work with a partner to practise the language you have studied in that unit. All the other work in each unit prepares you for this role play. It is an opportunity to activate what you have learned.

- **a reading text.** These are real English, from well-known professional English books. **Don't try to understand everything in these.** They will help you to learn how to read a text, even when you can't understand every word.

For extra practice you can use **Business Partners Workbook.** It has lots of extra exercises, and the answers are at the back of the book.

The **Cassette Tape** has clear recordings of all the dialogues and pronunciation exercises. Listening to the tape at home will help you to understand better. It will also help your pronunciation.

We hope you enjoy using **Business Partners.** Good Luck!

Pearson Brown   John Allison

UNIT 1: Canton Computers

Telephone language; Numbers; Business Vocabulary.

Switchboard	E.S.P. Ltd. Can I help you?
John	Could I speak to Mr Powell, please?
Switchboard	One moment please. *(pause)*
	I'm afraid his line's engaged.
John	I'll hold.
	(music)
Switchboard	Sorry to keep you waiting.
	(music)
Secretary	Mr Powell's office.
John	Can I speak to Mr Powell, please? It's John David from Canton Computers.
Secretary	I'm afraid he's in a meeting. Can I take a message?
John	Could you ask him to call John David– D-A-V-I-D. My number is 304 4577 and my extension is 557.
Secretary	John David. 340 4577 extension 557.
John	No, 304, not 340.
Secretary	Sorry, 304 4577 extension 557.
John	That's right.
Secretary	Right, thank you, Mr David. Goodbye.
John	Thank you. Goodbye.

1 Complete the box:

JOB	General Manager	Sales Representative
COMPANY		Canton Computers
TELEPHONE	273 2088	
EXTENSION	663	

2 Answer these questions about the dialogue. Sometimes you may not find the information you need in the dialogue.

1. What is the name of the company?
2. Who does Mr David want to speak to?
3. Who does he speak to (after the switchboard)?
4. What is the first problem?
5. What does Mr David say?
6. What is the second problem?
7. What is Mr David's job?
8. What is Mr David's phone number?

LANGUAGE STUDY

I'm afraid is used when your response is in some way unhelpful but the reason is outside your control. It means something like "I would help you if I could, but I can't".
What is the equivalent in your language?

3 Fill in the spaces by adding one of the following:

in   at   on   out of

1. I'm afraid she's .... a meeting.
2. I'm afraid he's .... holiday.
3. I'm afraid she's .... Grenoble today.
4. I'm afraid he's .... the factory.
5. I'm afraid she's .... the other line.
6. I'm afraid he's .... a trip all this week.
7. I'm afraid she's .... our Head Office today.
8. I'm afraid he's .... lunch.
9. I'm afraid he's tied up right now.

Say each sentence aloud, paying special attention to stress and intonation. In what situation do you think you might say each sentence?

Set One: Telephone Language

1 Find five words which can fill each column in this diagram. Choose words which you think will be useful to you.

Adjective		Noun
....		....
....	*call*	....
....		....
....		....
....		....

2 For each of these telephone expressions:

a. Who says it?
- the caller (C)
- the operator (O)
- the person receiving the call (R)

b. Underneath it, write the equivalent expression in your own language.

1. Can I help you?

2. Could I speak to (Mr Jones) please?

3. Who's calling, please?

4. This is (Mr Smith) from (Smith Computers).

5. One moment, please.

6. Hold the line please.

7. I'll put you through.

8. I'm afraid he's in a meeting.

9. Can I take a message?

10. Nick Jones speaking.

With a partner, prepare a dialogue to practise these expressions. After a few minutes, perform your dialogue.

3 Use one phrase from each section to form six mini-dialogues.

1. Could I speak to the Chairman's secretary please?
2. Good morning. Can I help you?
3. Is that Barker and Coby?
4. I'm afraid she's not in the office today.
5. Would you like him to call you back in a few minutes?
6. Could you speak up, please? I can hardly hear you.

a. Oh dear. Could I leave a message please?
b. No, I'll hang on.
c. Look, you hang up and I'll call you back.
d. Yes, I'll put you through.
e. Yes, I'd like to speak to Mr Hillier please.
f. No, I'm afraid you've got the wrong number.

Write your answers here:

1	2	3	4	5	6
d					

STUDY TIP

Before you listen to a tape, be sure your objective in listening is clear; decide if it is important to understand all the details or just the general idea. In most situations, the general idea is sufficient. Often you can understand 80% of the text easily, and that is usually enough. Don't worry about the rest!

4 Listening.

Mr Powell's secretary left him a note about John David's telephone call.

> John Davis from Kenton Computers rang. Can you call him back on 304 45788 ext. 577?

What problems will Mr Powell have when he returns the call?

Listen to Mr Powell trying to call Mr David. Does he succeed?

What most annoys you when you use the phone at work?

Have you ever had an amusing call made by mistake?

Set Two: Numbers

EXAMPLES

13 thir**teen** 30 **thir**ty
14 four**teen** 40 **for**ty
120 **one hun**dred and **twen**ty

1 Practise saying these numbers:

a. 22
b. 11
c. 28
d. 99
e. 52
f. 77
g. 38
h. 89
i. 12
j. 44
k. 30
l. 13
m. 40
n. 14
o. 50
p. 90
q. 70
r. 17
s. 19
t. 430
u. 550
v. 920
w. 210
x. 440
y. 220
z. 783

2 Listen to the tape and write the number you hear.

For some of the examples, you will hear a sentence. Write only the **number** the speaker says.

a. ....
b. ....
c. ....
d. ....
e. ....
f. ....
g. ....
h. ....
i. ....
j. ....
k. ....
l. ....
m. ....
n. ....
o. ....
p. ....
q. ....
r. ....
s. ....
t. ....
u. ....
v. ....
w. ....
x. ....
y. ....
z. ....

EXAMPLES

Give hotel room numbers like this:
347= three, four, seven   602= six, oh, two
and telephone numbers like this:
304 4577= three oh four, four five double seven

3 Say these:

a. Room 507, please.
b. 319, please.
c. I'm in room 903.
d. 247 629
e. 773940
f. 639009
g. 91345
h. 01 629 6699
i. 0240 12355

4 Listen to the tape. Write the numbers you hear. Sometimes they are in a complete sentence.

a. ....
b. ....
c. ....
d. ....
e. ....
f. ....
g. ....
h. ....
i. ....

5 Reading.

One week before the above conversation took place, Mr Powell received the following letter from Canton Computers.

CANTON COMPUTERS
8 The Broadway,
LONDON SW32 9BB

23 July

Dear Mr Powell,

<u>MMT 316 Laser Printer</u>

You placed an order with us for the above-mentioned machine on 12 June 1990. We promised delivery within one month.

There has been a slight delay in the arrival of the MMT 316 due to an industrial dispute in Germany. We expect normal shipping to resume within the next week or so and one of our sales staff will contact you as soon as we have more definite news.

We apologize for this delay which we are sure you will understand is outside our control.

Yours sincerely,

Michael Dexter

M.C. Dexter
Managing Director

True or False ?

1. Mr Powell has ordered a laser printer. ....
2. The printer has arrived. ....
3. Canton Computers is responsible for the delay. ....
4. John David is Mr Dexter's boss. ....

Set Three: Vocabulary

1 Fill in the missing letters.

1. Where goods are produced   F**T**Y   ....
2. Where finished goods are kept   W**EH*US*   ....
3. Where the workers have lunch   CA***EN   ....
4. Where the directors meet   BO****OO*   ....
5. Where the accountants work   **CO*N**   ....
6. Where the computer people work   E.*.*.   ....
7. Where the sales people 'work'   RE**AU**NT   ....
8. Where 'they' know nothing   HE** OF**C*   ....

2 Match the words:

1. financial   a. force
2. solid   b. sign
3. encouraging   c. share
4. market   d. relations
5. driving   e. foundation
6. industrial   f. market

Write your answers here:

1	2	3	4	5	6

"I'll have to put you on Hold, Mr Blacock, because Mr Jackson is on Hold with Mr Plunket who is on Hold with Mr Froshner who is on Hold with Mr Tilden who is on Hold with Mr Warburton who has stepped out of his office for a minute."

Set Four: The Alphabet

1 Say these:

a. E.C.
b. I.B.M.
c. B.B.C.
d. F.O.B.
e. O.E.C.D.
f. I.T.T.
g. T.W.A.
h. R.S.V.P.
i. I.C.I.
j. U.N.
k. K.L.M.
l. V.I.P.

What does each one stand for?

Can you give **one** place where you could see each one? (Be careful about the prepositions you use!)

**2 Spell your name and address.
Spell your company's name and address.**

....

....

3 Listen to the tape and write the names:

a. ....
b. ....
c. ....
d. ....
e. ....
f. ....
g. ....
h. ....
i. ....
j. ....
k. ....
l. ....

PAIR WORK – STUDENT 1

You are Mr Powell. After checking your files, you have discovered that you need to talk to John David, not Davis! Phone him at his office. If he is in, ask him when the MMT316 is to be delivered. If he is not available get him to ring back. You need the laser printer quickly. If there is still a problem with the MMT316, ask about other printers.

MODEL	MMT316
COST(£)	23,000
Copies p.m.	8

Your partner is the different voices you hear at the other end of the line.

PAIR WORK – STUDENT 2

First

You are the switchboard operator at Canton Computers.

Answer the telephone call from Mr Powell and connect him to Mr David's office.

Then

You are Mr David's secretary.

Mr David is in a meeting. Answer the telephone and take a message.

Then

You are John David. Phone back Mr Powell. Tell him that the strike in Germany is continuing and that there is very little chance of delivering the MMT316 before Christmas. Offer him the choice of some other models.

MODEL	MMT316	XY657	AEI988
COST(£)	23,000	26,599	27,689
Copies p.m.	8	12	14
Available	Jan	Now	Now

1 It's your business.

Have you had this type of problem?

Is telephoning in English difficult? Why?

2 Write.

Write a letter to confirm what you decided in your telephone conversation.

Set Five: Using Real Texts

STUDY TIP

This text has not been simplified. Do not try to understand every word. The text is only to help you to learn to read efficiently. It is best if you only do the suggested task.

Read the text and decide if:
These are 'rules' of how to answer the telephone.
These are 'rules' of how not to answer the telephone.

Rules for answering the telephone
Tenth rule - Don't let him get false ideas of his own importance.
Switchboard operator : 'Vers'l Nashn'l.
Bentley: Will you please put me through to the Managing Director?
Switchboard operator : Trying to connect you.
Secretary : Mr Gascoigne's office.
Bentley: I want to speak to Mr Gascoigne.
Secretary : Who is calling please?
Bentley: Is Mr Gascoigne there?
Secretary : Could I just have your name please?
Bentley: IS MR GASCOIGNE THERE?
Secretary : Could you just let me know what it's about?
Bentley: Is he there or is he not?
Secretary : Mr Gascoigne is a very busy man.
Bentley: So am I a very busy man. A very busy man. And I want to speak to Mr Gascoigne.
Secretary : Mr Gascoigne can't speak to everybody.
Bentley: I do not want Mr Gascoigne to speak to everybody. I want him to speak to me. Is he there?
Secretary : I'll just see if he's free.
(She puts the phone down, but makes no attempt to put Bentley through to Mr Gascoigne.)
Secretary : Hello? I'm afraid there's someone with him.
Bentley: Then will you tell him I want to speak to him?
Secretary : I can't interrupt, it's someone rather important. Could you just leave your name, and I'll get him to call you back?
Bentley: My name is Bentley of Parker and Gibbs and I have been trying to ....
Secretary : Righty-oh. We'll call you. Tarrah.
(She rings off and looks around for a pencil)
Eleventh rule - Always answer the next call before you make a note of the last one.
(The secretary starts to write 'Parker' on her pad when the phone rings again. She stops writing and answers it.)

(from **So You Think You Can Sell** by Video Arts)

Rewrite the conversation to show what a good secretary would say.

UNIT 2: The Expense Claim

Past simple; Questions and negatives;
Key vocabulary.

🔊	**John**	John David.
	Phil	It's Phil Buck from Accounts here. I received your expense claim a few minutes ago.
	John	Yes?
	Phil	And there are one or two things I'm not clear about. How long did you stay in France?
	John	Well, I went on Monday evening and I came back on Thursday morning.
	Phil	So three nights in a hotel. OK. And did you fly direct to Lyon?
	John	No I didn't have the time to book my ticket until last Saturday. I couldn't get a seat on the plane to Lyon so I flew to Paris and took the train down the next day.
	Phil	I see. And what hotel did you stay in?
	John	Well I tried to book a three star hotel but there was a big Trade Fair on and I had to go to a five star hotel.
	Phil	Why did you go?
	John	Well there was a problem with our agent there. So I went to find a solution.
	Phil	I hope you found one because the trip was very expensive.
	John	I did, don't worry. I sorted everything out.
	Phil	Look, because the expenses are over the limit, I'll have to get the Sales Director to approve them.
	John	Fine by me. Go ahead.

1 True (T), False (F) or Don't Know (?)

1. John went to France for two days. ....
2. Phil and John are talking on Friday. ....
3. John went on Monday morning. ....
4. He came back on Tuesday morning. ....
5. He flew direct to Lyon. ....
6. He stayed in a three star hotel. ....
7. The hotel cost 500 francs per night. ....
8. John found a solution to the problem with the agent. ....
9. Phil is happy and the problem is resolved. ....
10. The Sales Director reports to John. ....

2 Find expressions in the dialogue which mean:

a. I don't understand completely.

   ....

b. I have no objection.

   ....

c. I solved the problem completely.

   ....

LANGUAGE STUDY

We use the **Past Simple** to talk about events in the past which we see as finished. We can use it to talk about a point in time or a period of time.
It often occurs with time expressions such as **five days ago, yesterday, last Tuesday, in 1989, when I was at Business School.**

3 Practise saying these, paying attention to stress and intonation.

1. He phoned ten minutes ago.
2. I saw him at the Frankfurt Fair.
3. I had a meeting with her last Tuesday.
4. I joined the company in 1989.
5. I first met him when I was at Business School.
6. Did you reach your sales target last month?
7. I didn't see you at last week's meeting.
8. We didn't get the order after all.

Who would say these sentences? In what situations? Which are useful for **you**?

17

Set One: Past Simple – regular verbs

EXAMPLE
I received your expense claim a few minutes ago.

1 Mark each verb with one or more symbols.

Which of these verbs is normally associated with which department? (some verbs are used in more than one department)

S = Sales   P = Production   L = Personnel

1. work	7. appoint	13. want	19. return
2. recruit	8. negotiate	14. agree	20. visit
3. arrange	9. suggest	15. place	21. help
4. decide	10. photocopy	16. travel	22. accept
5. start	11. call back	17. phone	23. deliver
6. look up	12. design	18. ask	24. offer

2 Which of these verbs go naturally in this sentence:

Don't worry. I .... it yesterday.

3 Write the past form in the appropriate column.

These verbs all form their past by adding '-ed'. However, the pronunciation varies depending upon the last sound before the '-ed'. The first three have been done for you.

/ t /	/ d /	/ id /
worked	*arranged*	*recruited*

4 Reading.

Look at John's expense claim. Which items do you think are reasonable and which unreasonable.

EXPENSE CLAIM

NOTE: My briefcase was stolen during my return journey so I do not have the originals of my plane or train tickets.

Plane London – Paris return	£240
One night hotel Paris (bill attached)	£ 70
Dinner Paris (bill attached)	£ 37
Train Paris – Lyon return	£ 90
Two nights hotel in Lyon (bill attached)	£160
Dinner in hotel (alone) (bill lost)	£ 33
Dinner with agent (bill attached)	£130
Taxis etc.	£ 60
TOTAL	£820

---

5 Look at the following expense claims. Are they reasonable?

1. Two nights in a hotel for one afternoon meeting in Paris.
2. Dinner with a special client in a restaurant. Total bill of £150.
3. Two special economy class air tickets (for a salesman and his wife) costing in total £10 less than one business class ticket.

STUDY TIP

If you don't understand 20% of a newspaper article, you have a problem. If you don't understand 20% of a book, it is not so serious. To improve your vocabulary, read books without a dictionary. At first, there will be lots of things you don't understand, but just continue reading. Gradually you will understand more and more.

To improve your reading, choose a book that really interests you, that you really want to read. The level of difficulty is not important, but your motivation to read is essential.

Test your comprehension against your knowledge of the subject.

Set Two: Past Simple – Irregular verbs

EXAMPLE
I went on Monday evening and I came back on Thursday morning.

1 Complete the following table. The first one is done for you.

go	*went*
leave	....
meet	....
pay	....
ring	....
....	spoke
come	....
buy	....
....	brought
sell	....
think	....
fly	....
....	saw
rise	....
....	fell
begin	....
cost	....
....	put
take	....
tell	....

2 Use the verbs below to complete the newspaper article.

see,   start,   be,   be,   bring out,   return,   ask,
place,   put,   sell,   take over,   go,   have,   cost

In the early 1980's, Ellis .... the potential for home computers. Using standard components, he .... together his first computer, the YX30, and .... to market it in 1983. At first, he .... it through specialist electronic magazines. Then he .... advertisements in the 'quality' Sunday newspapers. It .... an immediate success.

Later that year, he .... the more powerful YX40. This .... colour graphics and .... £10 less than the YX30. However, there .... production problems. Many people .... their YX40 and .... for their money back. In 1985, Ellis .... bankrupt and Hampstead .... the rights to the YX30.

3 Use the verbs below to complete the report; you will need to use some of them twice.

rise, begin, buy, sell, cost, leave, meet, pay,
ring, speak, take, see, think, fly, tell

For once, my flight .... Heathrow on time! At Orly I .... a newspaper to look at prices, then .... a taxi downtown to .... with Mr Dupont, the agent. On the way, the taxi driver .... me the price of office space in Central Paris .... at least 15% last year. I .... Mr Dupont at the new "Business Tower" development and we .... offices on the ninth and seventeenth floors. I .... the seventeenth was the best, and .... to negotiate terms. I asked for a 10% reduction ; Mr Dupont .... his office and .... to his boss – we finally agreed on condition that we .... the furniture which is already in the office. I .... it's a good deal, as it will .... less than we .... 3 years ago in Marseilles. I .... home at 7pm ; my neighbour on the plane wanted to .... me all about his business – just as we landed I .... him a new computer system – so it was a good day's work!

4 Listening.

Phil Buck of Accounts is talking to the Sales Director. Listen to their conversation and write down their estimates of the real costs of each item.

Plane London – Paris return .... £

One night hotel Paris .... £

Dinner Paris .... £

Two nights hotel Lyon .... £

Dinner with agent .... £

Taxis etc. .... £

Set Three: Vocabulary

1 Find five words which can fill each column in this diagram.

Choose words which you think will be useful to you.

Verb	Adjective	
....	....	
....	....	*train*
....	....	
....	....	
....	....	

2 Find the missing words:

1. We set .... the subsidiary last year.
2. I decided to take .... his offer.
3. I decided to invest .... government stock.
4. I'm not interested .... your problems.
5. In Japan, Conilc are working .... a Japanese company.
6. I'm prepared to listen .... what you have to say.
7. I know all .... your problems, Malone.
8. I'm sure we can make a deal .... them.
9. I'm pleased .... what you've done.
10. We've taken .... 100 new workers since June.

3 Think of someone or something that is described by each of these words. Write the person or thing in the space.

1. shocking   ....   6. tricky   ....
2. promising   ....   7. painful   ....
3. convincing   ....   8. difficult   ....
4. hard-working   ....   9. impossible   ....
5. understanding   ....   10. serious   ....

Now make at least three sentences containing some of these words.

Set Four: Questions and Negatives

EXAMPLES
Did you fly direct to Lyon?
I didn't have the time to book my ticket until last Saturday.

---

1 Put this conversation into the correct sequence.

1. But they're urgent. I need them today.
2. Listen. We are still waiting for the SC112 you promised for last week.
3. Well they're not here. How did you send them?
4. Hello, Bob. It's Bill Elliot.
5. Did you send them 'Express'?

6. I didn't realize. Sorry, Bill. I'll send some more 'Express' today.
7. But we sent them on Friday.
8. No we didn't. We sent them parcel post.
9. By post.
10. Oh, hello Bill.

Write the correct sequence here: | 4 | | | | | | | | | |

---

2 Mark is talking to Sally about his business trip to Singapore. Look at Mark's answers and decide what questions Sally asked.

Sally	....
Mark	For a week.
Sally	....
Mark	Yes I really did. It was fantastic.
Sally	....
Mark	Of course I saw Barbara.
Sally	....
Mark	Yes. She said she was having a great time.
Sally	....
Mark	We went swimming in Barbara's pool.
Sally	....
Mark	Yes, of course. It was delicious.

PAIR WORK – STUDENT 1

You are the Sales Director. Question John about his expenses and decide if they are justified. Try to reduce them as much as possible.

PAIR WORK – STUDENT 2

You are John David. You went to France with your wife. She stayed with you in Paris and Lyon. Your real costs were:

Plane London – Paris return (Two economy fares of £85 each).	£170
One night hotel Paris (bill attached) (This was for a double room and two breakfasts. The cost for a single room is £62.)	£ 70
Dinner Paris (bill attached) (This was for two people but the bill doesn't show this.)	£ 37
Train Paris – Lyon return (Two second class tickets)	£ 90
Two nights hotel Lyon (bill attached) (This is for a double room (£10 per night extra) and includes £52 room service for two bottles of champagne.)	£160
Dinner in hotel (alone) (bill lost) (Dinner for two)	£ 33
Dinner with agent (bill attached) (He paid but you got a copy of the bill!)	£130
Taxis etc. (They really cost about £20 but you have no receipts.)	£ 60

The Sales Director is suspicious. Try to justify your original expense claim.

1 It's Your Business.

Are your expense claims always reasonable?

2 Write.

Write a memo to the salesman.

STUDY TIP

Sometimes we don't need to read a text in detail if we just want certain information. Use key words to help you "scan" a text to find the essential information ; read only the sentences where you see a key word.

Set Five: Using Real Texts

1 Match the phrase to the explanation.

1. Took early retirement.
2. Early retirement because of ill health.
3. He will continue on a part-time consultancy basis.
4. Leaving for personal reasons.
5. Resigned.
6. His departure is deeply regretted.

a. The company is very sorry that he is leaving.
b. Stop working before the usual age to retire because you are sick.
c. He will continue to give advice to the company.
d. He is leaving his job because of personal problems.
e. Stop working before the usual age to retire.
f. He has sent a letter to his company to say he wants to give up his job.

Write your answers here:

1	2	3	4	5	6

The following text makes fun of the sort of 'kind' language sometimes used to explain why people have left a company.

When People Leave the Company:

"Took early retirement." — Luckily he was just old enough for people to believe he wasn't sacked.

"Early retirement because of ill health." — He was making us sick.

"He decided to leave to pursue his private business interests." — He was sacked.

"Left by mutual agreement." — He was sacked, but we paid him some money not to make a fuss about it.

"He will continue on a part-time consultancy basis." — He was sacked but was not a bad chap.

"Leaving for personal reasons." — He was sacked and we couldn't stand him anyway.

"Resigned." — Guilty of at least fraud.

"His departure is deeply regretted." — It cost us a fortune to get rid of him, and we regret losing the money.

(from **The Extremely Serious Guide to Business** by Keith Ray)

Did you find the text funny? Does your company do this?
Underline all the verbs in the past simple. Make sure you know what they mean.

UNIT 3: Stepniewski

Polite requests; Answering requests; Eating out.

Receptionist Good evening, madam.
Guest Good evening. My name is Stepniewski. I have a room reserved.
Receptionist I'm sorry, madam. Could you spell your name, please?
Guest Yes, of course. S T E P N I E W S K I.
Receptionist Ah yes. Room 509. A single room for three nights with English breakfast, is that right?
Guest Yes that's correct.
Receptionist Would you mind waiting one moment whilst I make your key?
Guest Sorry? I'm afraid I don't understand.
Receptionist We have a computerized system for our locks. The combination changes for each guest so you can be sure your room is totally safe.
Guest Ah I see.
Receptionist Here you are, madam. Room 509 on the fifth floor. The lift is right behind you.
Guest Thank you.
Receptionist Do you intend to eat here this evening, madam?
Guest Yes.
Receptionist Well the restaurant closes at 9.30, madam, so I suggest you leave us to take up your luggage and that you go there right away.
Guest Right-oh. Thank you. I'll do that.

1 Answer these questions:

1. What is the guest's name?
2. How long is she staying?
3. Is she alone or with her husband?
4. Does she want English or Continental breakfast?
5. What is unusual about the key?
6. What is the number of the room?
7. What time is it?
8. Does the guest go directly to her room?

2 Explain the meaning of:

a. Is that right?
b. Right behind you
c. Right away
d. Right-oh

LANGUAGE STUDY

In the dialogue, underline where the receptionist makes a request to Ms Stepniewski.
Could you is followed by the infinitive without 'to'.
Would you mind is followed by the 'ing' form of the verb. It means "would you object to" so if you have no objection, you answer **'No'**.
If you do object, you usually explain why you object.

3 Say the following sentences with special attention to stress and intonation.

1. Could you tell me why you're leaving?
2. Could you lend me a hand, please?
3. Could you do that at once, please?
4. Would you mind making less noise?
5. Would you mind working overtime tonight?
6. Would you mind telling me why it took so long?

In what situation do you think you might say or hear each sentence?

Set One: Making Polite Requests

EXAMPLES
Could you spell your name please?
Would you mind waiting a moment, please?

1 Who would make these requests?

Practise saying them paying attention to stress and intonation.

1. Could you tell me how much it costs?
2. Could you tell me where Mr Smith's office is?
3. Could you tell me if your price includes VAT?
4. Could you tell me if you have the X230 in stock?
5. Could you get us two black coffees please, Barbara?
6. Would you mind opening your briefcase?
7. Would you mind telling me who your supplier is?
8. Would you mind leaving us for five minutes?

2 Make polite requests:

1. You want to know how to spell 'personnel'.
   ....
2. You want to know how to pronounce 'productivity'.
   ....
3. You want someone to speak more slowly.
   ....
4. You want someone to repeat what they have said.
   ....
5. You want someone to help you.
   ....

3 Find five words which can fill each column in this diagram.

Choose words which you think will be useful to you.
All the phrases should go in front of the word **restaurant**, for example, eg.
Shall we try the local Indian restaurant.

Adjective	Nationality	
....	....	*restaurant*
....	....	
....	....	
....	....	
....	....	

4 Listening.

Ms Stepniewski is talking to the hotel telephone operator. Listen and answer these questions.

1. What number do you dial to get an outside line? ....

2. What is the code number for Sweden? ....

3. What is the cost per minute of a call to Sweden?

   from 9 pm to 8 am ....

   from 8 am to 1 pm ....

   from 1 pm to 9 pm ....

4. What time does the guest want her morning call? ....

5. Does she want tea or coffee? ....

6. What newspaper does she want?
   The Times, The Daily Telegraph, The Independent ....

Check with the text in the back of your book (page 153). Underline the examples of polite requests made by the operator and by the guest.

5 Decide what to say in the following situations:

1. You are talking to the telephone operator at XYZ Ltd. You want to speak to Mr Elphee in Sales.

   ....

2. Ask Mr Elphee when the next shipment will be sent.

   ....

3. You want Mr Elphee to send you a copy of invoice 667743.

   ....

4. Ask Mr Walker's secretary if you can speak to him.

   ....

5. She says Mr Walker is absent. Ask when he will be back.

   ....

6. Ask if you can leave a message.

   ....

Set Two: Answering Requests

EXAMPLES

Could you spell your name, please?
- Yes, of course. (agree)
- Sorry, I don't know the English alphabet. (refuse and explain)

Would you mind waiting a minute, please?
- No, of course not. (agree)
- I'm afraid I can't. I'm in a hurry. (refuse and explain)

1 Match the request with the answer.

1. Could you give me a lift? My car has broken down.
2. This photocopier isn't working. Could you give me a hand?
3. Would you mind working on Sunday morning?
4. Could you tell me the time?
5. Could you answer the phone?
6. Would you mind finding somewhere else to talk?

a. It's my office too, I'm afraid, but we'll try to be quieter.
b. Sorry, I'm busy. You do it.
c. I'm afraid I can't. I always go to church on Sundays.
d. Sure. It's 11 o'clock.
e. Of course, I'll pick you up at seven.
f. Of course. I don't know why they don't get a new one.

Write your answers here:

1	2	3	4	5	6

2 Answer these requests.

1. Could you come back at 5.00? (You have another appointment)
   ....
2. Could you come back after five o' clock? (Agree)
   ....
3. Could you phone me at 6.00? (You finish work at 5.30)
   ....
4. Would you mind changing our appointment to Friday? (Agree)
   ....
5. Would you mind moving our appointment to Friday? (You're going to Paris on Friday.)
   ....
6. Would you mind working late tonight? (You're going to the theatre.)
   ....

3   Reading.

This is the menu from the hotel restaurant. What items are most suitable for:
a. someone who loves fish?
b. a vegetarian?
c. someone watching their weight?

Kate's Kitchen

Cream of mushroom soup   Grapefruit Cocktail
Avocado with crab   Honeydew melon
Prawn Cocktail   Home-made paté

Fried plaice with lemon
Trout with almonds
Mixed seafood in a white wine, cream and mushroom sauce
Roast duckling with orange sauce
Turkey supreme
Grilled fillet steak
Roast beef with Yorkshire Pudding
Spinach quiche

French fried potatoes   Jacket potatoes
Onion rings   Baby carrots
French beans   Garden peas

Peach melba
Sherry trifle
Home-made apple pie with cream or ice-cream
Lemon cheesecake
Black forest gateau

Stilton with port
Cheeseboard

---

4   Practise ordering a meal.

A table for (one), please.
I'd like to start with (the soup).
To follow I'll have (the plaice).
We'd like a bottle of (the house white).
Could I have the bill, please?

Set Three: Vocabulary

1 Match the verb to the noun:

1. book
2. set up
3. make
4. open
5. break into
6. face

a. a factory
b. competition
c. a market
d. a deal
e. a room
f. a business

Write your answers here:

1	2	3	4	5	6

2 Look at the picture of a hotel room. On the list below number each item which is numbered in the picture.

.... bath	.... shower	.... toilet
.... bedside table	.... radio	.... TV
.... light	.... fridge	.... light switch
.... bulb	.... shaving socket	.... hook

32

Set Four: Vocabulary

1 Which verbs can go with which nouns? (More than one may be possible.)

For many people, the worst part of going away on a business trip is finding something to do in the evening. Here is a list of things you could do in the evening.

go to	the hotel restaurant
take in	a show
see	a night club
read	a film
try	a play
eat in	television
watch	a football match
have	a good book
visit	a drink
catch up with	some local food
	my work
	an early night

STUDY TIP

To memorise vocabulary, you have to use it. Decide which words are important for you. You will find it difficult to remember words which are not immediately useful. Try to make **your own,** personal sentences with vocabulary you want to learn.

PAIR WORK – STUDENT 1

You are a hotel guest. Ask the porter about restaurants and theatres. You want to spend no more than £40 – £50 for the evening.

PAIR WORK – STUDENT 2

You are the Hotel Porter. The guests ask your advice about restaurants and shows. Most of these give you commission. Help your partner to organize their evening. Try to make as much commission as possible.

Theatre/ Clubs

QUEENS   'West End Story'   musical   8% commission

                          Seats £20 £10 £5

REGAL   'Naughty Nites'   striptease   15% commission

                Show £15   Show plus dinner £50

ROYAL   'Hamlet'   Shakespeare 1% commission

                          Seats £20 £10 £5

Restaurants

CHINESE	£25 meal	£5 commission
ITALIAN	£35 meal	£5 commission
TRADITIONAL ENGLISH	£40 meal	no commission
FRENCH	£50 meal	no commission

1 It's your business.

Are hotel porters really like this?

Is your language more polite or more direct than English?

When you are away on business, how do you like to spend your evenings?

2 Write.

Write a letter reserving a room in a hotel.

Set Five: Using Real Texts

STUDY TIP

This text has not been simplified. Do not try to understand every word. The text is only to help you to learn to read efficiently. It is best if you do only the suggested tasks.

1 **Put a cross (X) beside the possible advantages of silence that the author mentions.**

1. You can think about your holidays.
2. You can learn more about the client.
3. You do not tell the client things you do not want them to know.
4. You will impress the client more than by speaking too much.
5. You will not get so tired.
6. The client will force you to speak.
7. You can think about what you are doing.
8. If the client does not speak, they cannot commit themselves.
9. The client may tell you things they do not want you to know.

A lot has been written about the use of silence in selling. For good reason. There comes a point in almost any sales pitch where the other person should be talking, and there comes a point in almost any sales pitch where *no one* should be talking. It's pretty hard to get to either point if you don't know when to be silent.

Silence has so many different selling applications. If you stop talking and start listening you might actually learn something, and even if you don't you'll have a chance to collect your thoughts. Silence is what keeps you from saying more than you need to – and makes the other person want to say more than he means to. Knowing when to remain silent can strongly influence the impression you make on others. And furthermore, it's impossible to get a commitment out of someone, if that person can't get a word in edgeways.

The tactical use of silence serves one of two purposes. It either lets the other person talk, or forces the other person to talk.

(from **What They Don't Teach You at Harvard Business School** by Mark H. McCormack)

Do you agree with the author?

UNIT 4: York

Present perfect; Adverbs of time; Vocabulary.

🔘	**Graham**	Graham Powell speaking.
	Chris	Hello, Graham. It's Chris Stepniewski here. I haven't received your report yet on the Munich Project.
	Graham	Sorry Chris. I've been off sick for the last couple of days. I've just come back today. But I've nearly finished it. It will be in the post tonight, I promise.
	Chris	OK Graham. Has Brian Abbotts spoken to you about the problem in the York production unit?
	Graham	No. What's wrong?
	Chris	They've stopped work. There's a tanker driver strike. It started two days ago and they've already run out of diesel for the generators.
	Graham	Have you ever heard anything so ridiculous?
	Chris	Exactly. I told them years ago to get a back-up system – build a reserve tank or something – but they've never done anything about it.
	Graham	Some people never listen, do they? Well, I'll get on with this report. I'll get it off tonight or tomorrow at the latest.
	Chris	OK. See you soon.

1   **Answer these questions:**

1. Why is the Munich Project report late?
2. Does Graham already know about the problem in York?
3. What is the problem?
4. Did Chris anticipate the problem?
5. When will Graham finish the report?
6. When will he post the report?

2   **Find words and expressions which mean:**

1. to be away from work ill
2. to have used all your supply
3. a second system to replace the first when it goes wrong
4. to make progress
5. to send

LANGUAGE STUDY

The **Present Perfect** is formed using 'have' and the Past Participle. It is a present tense and it is used to **look back** from the present to the past. There is always something **Now** which makes the speaker look back to an earlier event. Can you see that with these examples:

Oh, you've had a haircut.
You don't need to write to Peter. I've already spoken to him on the phone.

Underline the examples of the **Present Perfect** in the text and discuss with your teacher why the speaker chose to use the Present Perfect and not another tense.

3   Find five words which can fill each column in this diagram. Choose words which you think will be useful to you.

Verb	Adjective	
		order

Set One: Present Perfect

EXAMPLES
I've just come back today.
They've already run out of diesel.
I haven't received your report yet.

1 Make a sentence about what Simon has already done, has just done and hasn't yet done.

It is now 3.30. Look at Simon's 'to do' list:

Write report on meeting with ZTY.
Phone Jim Simpson about the new contract
Phone John Lauder about Kuwait.
Phone bank about personal loan.
Telex Hong Kong about the shipping delay.
See Frank Howard about overtime
See union representative for weekly meeting.
Check expense claims.

This is what Simon has done so far today:

9.00	Arrived. Discussed personal problem with secretary
9.20	Opened post
9.50	Started writing report
10.00	Telephone call from Chairman
10.30	Continued writing report
10.40	Telephone call from Chief Accountant
11.10	Continued writing report
11.20	Stopped writing to prepare meeting with union
11.30	Meeting with union
12.30	Lunch
1.30	Continued report
1.40	Telephone call from Chairman
2.35	Continued report
3.15	Finished report
3.20	Phoned John Lauder

2 Look at your 'to do' list for today/this week. Make sentences about what you have already done and haven't done yet.

3 Complete the dialogue:

Roger   Why are you looking so happy?

Patricia I .... We ....
              the Jacquot contract.   (just hear) (get)

Roger   The Jacquot contract! Well done!

Patricia Yes, They .... all our proposals.   (accept)

Roger   What? Even the payment at thirty days?

Patricia Well, no. They .... for payment
              at sixty days.   (ask)

Roger   Even so, that's great. I'd better tell the MD.

Patricia Don't worry. I .... him.   (already tell)

Can you always see something **now** which makes the speaker look back, when the present perfect is used?

4 Listening.

The strike at the York production unit lasted three weeks. Now it is over and normal production has resumed. There is a large backlog in shipments from York to Bath. Listen to the phone conversation between Freddy Hutton, General Manager of the York production unit and Brian Abbotts, General Manager of the assembly unit in Bath. Complete the chart.

Part	Quantity	
	Already sent	**Not sent yet**
AB122	....	....
AB132	....	....
AD122	....	....
GJ134	....	....
GK122	....	....
JK112	....	....
YZ113	....	....
YZ130	....	....

Set Two: Present Perfect with *for/since*

1 Can these expressions be used with for, since or both?

10 years	1978	2 months
6 weeks	2 February	my birthday
5 minutes	the war	last summer
a long time	I was at school	10 hours
ages	Christmas	the summer

2 Cross out the incorrect sentence and write the correct sentence in the space provided.

One sentence in each group is incorrect.

1. We've sold ten thousand units so far this year.

   This is the first time we exceed our objectives by 50%.

   We've never had such a good result before.

   ....

2. Our turnover generally increases by about 5% per annum.

   Of course our targets have increased every year since 1973.

   This year they increase by 20% compared to last year.

   ....

3. The market has expanded considerably since we launched our "A" range.

   Since that time, our total staff has tripled.

   The majority of our salesmen have only worked for us since one year.

   ....

4. For about six months we don't advertise at all.

   Our order book is full for the next three months.

   We have had to employ temporary staff for a year.

   ....

5. The management have promised us a bonus at the end of the year.

   We haven't already received our overtime payments.

   However, they have already set up a profit-sharing scheme.

   ....

3 Reading.

Brian Abbotts received the following fax from Head Office in Barcelona.

MEMO

Brian,

We need full details of your current position ASAP.

Freddy Hutton says the strike has ended and that everything is back to normal and running smoothly. Could you confirm this?

Are supplies now arriving normally from York? Have you had any more difficulties? Have you caught up the backlog?

You must keep us better informed about your problems. We haven't heard from you for over a week. Fax us back today!

Regards,

Chris

Chris

True, false or don't know?

1. Chris needs details from Brian urgently. ....
2. Chris has spoken recently to Freddy. ....
3. The strike ended two days ago. ....
4. Freddy has told Chris that there are big problems. ....
5. Brian faxed Chris three days ago. ....
6. Brian and Chris are good friends. ....

"A word of advice, Arthur: no-one has ever solved his problems by running away."

Set Three: Vocabulary

1 Which of these words are concerned with employment (E) and which with finance (F)?

1. union ....
2. personnel ....
3. depreciation ....
4. shop stewards ....
5. profit-sharing ....
6. assets ....
7. benefits in kind ....
8. balance sheet ....
9. management ....
10. strike ....

2 Positive or negative?

How do you feel about each of these?

1. the closed shop
2. government arbitration
3. unions
4. an incomes policy
5. worker directors
6. strikes
7. management restaurants
8. shop stewards
9. flexi-time
10. right-to-work laws

3 Match the words:

1. make
2. see
3. foot
4. offer
5. achieve
6. predict

a. the future
b. a loss
c. results
d. opportunities
e. a range of products
f. the bill

Write your answers here:

1	2	3	4	5	6

Set Four: Present Perfect with *ever/never/always*

1 Complete these sentences:

1. I've always wanted to ....

2. I've never wanted to ....

3. I've never ....

4. If you've never ....
   .... you've never lived!

2 Are you a model employee?

1. Have you ever worn jeans to work? — Yes/No
2. Have you ever 'overestimated' your expenses? — Yes/No
3. Have you ever stayed at home 'ill' when you were OK? — Yes/No
4. Have you ever shouted at your boss? — Yes/No
5. Have you ever had a sleep in your office after lunch? — Yes/No
6. Have you ever made a personal long-distance call from work? — Yes/No
7. Have you ever put a foreign coin in the coffee machine? — Yes/No
8. Have you ever gone on strike? — Yes/No

Results		
7-8	YES	*Have you still got a job?*
5-6	YES	*You must work in Marketing.*
3-4	YES	*You must want to work in Marketing.*
1-2	YES	*Don't play poker with the people in Marketing.*
0	YES	*You must be an Accountant.*

PAIR WORK – STUDENT 1

You are Freddy Hutton, General Manager of the York production unit. These are the final figures for parts shipped at the end of week 17. Telephone Brian Abbotts and give him the information about what has been sent and what has not been sent.

Part	already sent	not sent yet
AB122	20 000	0
AB132	19 000	1 000
AD122	10 000	10 000
GJ134	12 000	3 000
GK122	19 500	500
JK112	20 000	0
YZ113	30 000	10 000
YZ130	40 000	0

PAIR WORK – STUDENT 2

You are Brian Abbotts, General Manager of the Bath assembly unit. You have already received some parts (see the chart below). You know that York have probably sent some more parts which have not arrived yet and that there will be other parts which they are going to send but have not sent yet.

Part	already received	in transit	not sent yet
AB122	15 000		
AB132	19 000		
AD122	7 000		
GJ134	10 000		
GK122	9 500		
JK112	20 000		
YZ113	13 000		
YZ130	30 000		

When Freddy Hutton telephones you, complete the rest of your chart.

1 It's Your Business.

Have you ever had problems because one of your suppliers had production difficulties?

Have you ever had a strike and been unable to supply your customers?

Complete the following sentences honestly and naturally about your own business.

1. We've looked at the possibility of ....
2. We've had a lot of trouble with ....
3. We've decided to ....
4. We've started to .... but we haven't got very far yet.
5. And we haven't even started to ....

2 Write.

Write the telex Brian Abbotts sends to confirm the telephone call.

Set Five: Using Real Texts

1   What do you think is the main purpose of this text?

When Describing the Business Year:

"It's been a fairly average year."	We made a loss.
"It's been a challenging year."	We made disastrous losses.
"We made disastrous losses."	We did rather well, but there's no reason why we should let everyone know about it.
"It's been a bad first quarter."	It's coming round to annual pay-talk time, and we don't want to pay the workers any more.
"It's been a good first quarter."	The rest of the year is going to be a disaster, so it doesn't really matter what we tell the unions now.
"We achieved our plan."	We didn't really achieve our plan, but who believes in plans anyway?
"The market has been lively."	We've been screwed to the wall by our competitors."
"Things are looking up."	We're at the bottom of the abyss, so nothing could look down.
"We've been investing in future capacity."	The new factory was a mistake.
"There appears to be excess capacity in the industry."	Everyone else has made the same mistake too.

(from **The Extremely Serious Guide to Business** by Keith Ray)

Did you find the text funny?

Does your company communicate like this?

Most of the verbs in the text are in the present perfect. Why is this?

UNIT 5: Manchester

Present simple, Present continuous;
Adverbs of frequency; Important words.

The Financial Director of Canton Computers is talking to Phil Buck of Accounts.

F. Director Phil, I'd like you to do a check up on procedures at our Manchester branch.
Phil Of course, Bob. What's the problem?
F. Director Well, as you know, all branches submit a financial report every month. Manchester usually send in their report at least a week late and they often make mistakes in it. And when we telephone them for information, nobody seems to know what's going on.
Phil Who's the Chief Accountant?
F. Director John Baxter. He's rarely in his office. He never returns my calls either.
Phil What about the General Manager?
F. Director Oh him! Joe Stanthorpe is an engineer by training and he gives John Baxter a completely free hand. He says he's more interested in making a profit than in paperwork.
Phil Well, I'd better pay them a visit. I'm writing the report on the Milan subsidiary but I can probably clear Monday and Tuesday of next week, if it's really urgent.
F. Director Thanks, Phil. I'm sure you can find a solution.

1 True, False or Not Sure?

1. The problem with the Manchester accounting department is temporary. ....
2. The Finance Director anticipates no change in the behaviour of the Chief Accountant in Manchester. ....
3. The Managing Director in Manchester controls the Chief Accountant well. ....
4. Phil is writing the report on Milan and speaking to the Finance Director at the same moment. ....
5. Phil can visit Manchester next week. ....

2 Underline expressions in the text which mean:

1. to arrange for Monday and Tuesday to be free of all other work
   ....
2. to let someone do what he wants
   ....
3. to make an assessment
   ....

LANGUAGE STUDY

We use the **Present Simple** to talk about present situations we see as long-term or permanent.

We use the **Present Continuous** to talk about present situations we see as short-term or temporary.

In the dialogue, underline the verbs in the present and decide why the speaker chooses that particular form.

3 Practise saying them with the correct stress and intonation.

1. I visit Paris three or four times a year.
2. He's a man who works hard and plays hard.
3. I don't like that idea very much.
4. She doesn't want you to do it.
5. I'm working very long hours at the moment.
6. She's thinking of changing her job.

In what situation do you think you might say these?

STUDY TIP

All English words of two syllables or more have a strong accent on one syllable. Make sure when you learn a new word you know where the stress is – mark it like this : **pronunciation.**

Stressing words wrongly makes you more difficult to understand than having a foreign accent.

Set One: Present Forms

EXAMPLES

Manchester usually send in their report one week late. (Example A)

I'm writing the report on the Milan subsidiary. (Example B)

1 Are these sentences like Example A or Example B?

1. The company is losing money for the first time.
2. I admire the President.
3. Mr Lewis often goes to Germany on business.
4. Sales often drop in August.
5. I report to Head Office every month.
6. Japan is usually a very difficult market to enter.
7. I don't often finish work before 6.00 so an early finish is a nice change.
8. I read the F.T. first thing every morning.
9. He is visiting Singapore for the Trade Fair.
10. I'm still working on the report but you can have it tomorrow.

2 Put in the correct present form of the verb indicated.

Sometimes both forms are possible but with slightly different meanings.

1. IBM .... computers. (make)
2. IBM .... a revolutionary new portable computer. (develop)
3. The dollar .... against the pound. (rise)
4. The dollar .... at 1.7 to the pound. (stand)
5. EIL .... 10% of the market. (have)
6. EIL .... 100 employees redundant. (make)
7. Mr Hill .... his report this week. (write)
8. Mr Hill often .... his reports .... late. (send in)
9. Business .... (boom)
10. Sales .... steadily. (grow)

3 Discuss

What do you do in your job?

What are you working on at the moment?

4 Write four nouns which can follow each of these words. One is done to help you.

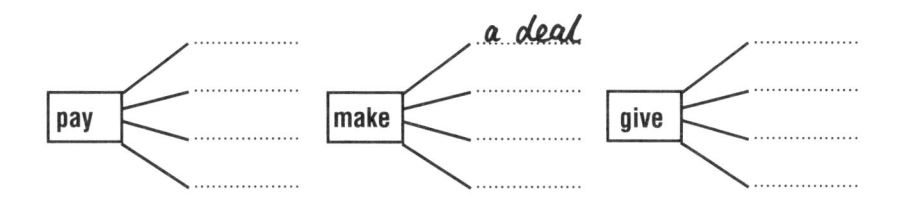

pay ....
....
....
....

make ..a deal
....
....
....

give ....
....
....
....

5 Write four things you are:

good at	not very good at
....	....
....	....
....	....
....	....

We usually say **I'm not very good at Spanish,** not **I'm bad at Spanish.**

6 Listening.

Phil is discussing the problems in the Accounting Department with John Baxter, the Chief Accountant.

Answer these questions:
1. Is Phil going to write a favourable report?
2. How many problems has he noted?
3. How many people work in Accounts Receivable?
4. How many are usually absent?
5. What is the main reason for these absences?
6. Is Accounts Receivable efficient?
7. Is Accounts Payable efficient?
8. Why does Mr Baxter pay the suppliers so early?

What are the opposites of these words:

favourable .... efficient .... early ....

Set Two: Adverbs of Frequency

EXAMPLES
He's rarely in his office.
He never returns my calls.
Branches submit a financial report every month.

1 Arrange these expressions in order of frequency. Use 1 for the most frequent and so on.

First Group

| never .... | often .... | sometimes .... | occasionally .... |
| always .... | rarely .... | usually .... | frequently .... |

Second Group

twice a week	....	every week	....
daily	....	monthly	....
every other month	....	annually	....
every six months	....	three times a year	....

Where do these expressions usually come in a sentence?

2 Write some true statements about yourself and your company using these expressions.

3 Are you a Workaholic? Complete each sentence using one of:

usually (5)   often (4)   sometimes (3)   don't often (2)   never (1)

1. I .... arrive at work before 9.00.
2. I .... leave work after 6.00.
3. I .... read technical magazines in the evening.
4. I .... take work home at weekends.
5. I .... fail to do all the work on my 'to do' list.
6. I .... think about my work when I am at home.
7. I .... have sleepless nights because of problems at work.
8. I .... continue working when I am too tired to do it well.

Results

32-40   You show signs of being a workaholic! Slow down!
17-31   You are a typical manager! Try to relax more.
11-16   You seem to be well organized.
8-10   Perhaps you are too relaxed

4   Reading.

This is an extract from the draft of a report prepared by Phil. He has submitted this draft to Joe Stanthorpe, the Managing Director of EIL Manchester, for his comments.

Read the report and answer these questions:
1. Why can't you talk to Mr Baxter at 2 o'clock?
2. Who is the real boss of the department?
3. What is the problem with Ms Brown?
4. Do you think morale in the department is good?
5. Does the company have a good system of credit control?

REPORT ON 2 DAY VISIT TO ACCOUNTING DEPARTMENT OF EIL Manchester HIGHLY CONFIDENTIAL

I visited the above department during Week 17. I observed the following:

1. Mr Baxter, the Chief Accountant, rarely supervises the work of his subordinates. He leaves that to his assistant, Ms Brown. He appears to sit in his office and do very little. He is currently preparing the budget for next year but he doesn't appear to be doing very much work. He sometimes goes out to lunch at 12 and comes back after 3.
2. Ms Brown, the Assistant Chief Accountant, really runs the department. However, she is expecting a baby in six months and she is not certain if she will continue her job after that. None of the clerks seems capable of replacing her.
3. Many clerks arrive late and leave early. Absenteeism is high.
4. Presently, customers are paying on average at 90 days (due to absenteeism) but suppliers are being paid at 40 days.
5. The Managing Director does not control the Department. He delegates all his authority to Mr Baxter.

Further Action: I have submitted a copy of this report to Joe Stanthorpe, the General Manager. We are meeting on Friday, 27 November to discuss it.

---

5   Which of the above problems are short-term and which long-term?

1. short-term / long-term
2. short-term / long-term
3. short-term / long-term
4. short-term / long-term
5. short-term / long-term

Set Three: Present forms

1 Complete the questions with these words.

Auxiliaries do   does
Full verbs   live earn think start work
             have take mean   enjoy pronounce

1. Where .... you ....?
2. What time .... you .... work?
3. Where .... you .... lunch?
4. .... you .... your job?
5. How long .... it .... you to come to work?
6. What .... 'turnover' ....?
7. How .... you .... 'key'?
8. How much .... Pat ....?
9. .... she .... very hard?
10. What .... you .... of him?

2 Match the questions to these answers:

a. I'm not very sure.
b. I think so.
c. In the staff canteen.
d. Just outside Birmingham.
e. Yes, of course.
f. About 30 minutes.
g. It's the total sales for the period.
h. At 8.00.
i. About 9000 francs a month.
j. It sounds like 'he'.

Write your answers here:

1	2	3	4	5	6	7	8	9	10

3 Who does what?

Read the information about Giles, Jeremy and Caroline. One is in advertising; one is a bureaucrat at Head Office and one is self-employed. Who does what?

Caroline usually starts work at 8.00 am.
Giles usually finishes work at 5.00 pm.
Jeremy thinks a lot and draws well.
Caroline does a lot of things every day.
Giles often walks round with pieces of paper in his hand.
Jeremy works when he feels creative.
Nobody knows what Giles does.

Jeremy is .... Caroline is .... Giles is ....

Set Four: Vocabulary

EXAMPLES
All branches submit a financial report every month.
He says he's more interested in making a profit than in paperwork.
I'd better pay them a visit.

1 Which of these verbs can you use with 'report', 'profit', 'visit'?
   (some verbs can be used with more than one noun)

make,   write,   send in,   read,   ask for,   take,   double
   reduce,   receive,   have,   increase,   pay,   submit

....
.... } a report
....

....
.... } a profit
....

....
.... } a visit
....

PAIR WORK – STUDENT 1

You are Phil. Look again carefully at the report (see pg. 51) you have prepared and at your notes on your meeting with Mr Baxter (Listening page 49). Decide in detail on the changes you feel should be implemented.

When you have finished, discuss the report with Joe Stanthorpe.

PAIR WORK – STUDENT 2

You are Joe Stanthorpe, General Manager, Manchester branch. You have read Phil's report (pg. 51) but feel he hasn't understood all the problems.

In particular,

1. You are thinking of leaving. You have been offered a new job. You don't think it reasonable to start to make major changes.
2. The Chief Accountant visits his wife in hospital every lunch-time.
3. Your biggest supplier is asking you to pay at 30 days, as in the purchase agreement. He may cut off your supplies unless you respect the agreement. This would be a disaster for your company.

How does this information help you to answer the points made in Phil's report. What changes, if any, do you feel should be made to the department?

When you have finished, discuss the report with Phil.

1 It's your business.

What does your company do when employees have personal problems? Should employees be allowed time off when their children are ill?

2 Writing.

Write the report prepared by Phil after his discussion with the Managing Director.

STUDY TIP

"To skim" is to travel very fast over the surface ; before you read a text in detail, read very very quickly or "diagonally" to discover
    a. if it's interesting
    b. which parts are most interesting
    c. the general ideas of the text
Then you can use the information you have "skimmed" to test your understanding when you read in detail.

Set Five: Using Real Texts

STUDY TIP

This text has not been simplified. Do not try to understand every word.
The text is only to help you to learn to read efficiently.
It is best if you only do the suggested tasks.

1 **What is the main message of this text?**

a. Office workers work less than manual workers.
b. The time when you read is called prime time.
c. Use your prime time well.
d. Do not read newspapers at work.
e. Everybody works best in the morning.

PROTECTING PRIME TIME

If you are an office worker, there are far greater peaks and valleys in your achievement level than there are for manual workers. Chances are, most of your work gets done in only a portion of your working day, the time we might designate prime time.

For most people, the first couple of hours of the day are prime time. But many of us ignore this fact and spend those hours doing routine tasks: reading the morning mail (which seldom contains top-priority items), reading periodicals, glancing through the morning newspaper, making routine phone calls, and so on. It doesn't take much thought to see the waste this entails; the best time of day should be spent on the things that matter most, the things that require top energy, complete alertness, greatest creativity.

So schedule your one or two highest-priority tasks for the day in your prime time, and work at the low-priority tasks when you can.

(from **Getting Things Done** by Edwin C. Bliss)

How easy is it to use your prime time efficiently?

UNIT 6: The Trade Fair

Present continuous for the future;
(be) going to; business vocabulary.

Thomas Could you look at this, Graham? I received it this morning.
Grant (*reading*) The PC Times Show. Not another exhibition! Look, the promotional budget for next year has already been decided. We're exhibiting at the Frankfurt, Milan and Paris Fairs. That's all. We don't have the money or the man-power to go to any more. And there's no point in taking a risk on a new show run by a new magazine and organized at such short notice.
Thomas Wait a moment. Remember that PC Times is owned by that Canadian chap who owns all those newspapers and the satellite TV network. It says in the brochure that they're going to give the exhibition maximum coverage. They're going to have special features in the newspapers and magazines and they're going to produce a TV programme from the show every night featuring some of the products from the show.
Grant When and where is it?
Thomas They're holding it at the Birmingham N.E.C. in the last week in March.
Grant Let's see. Milan is taking place in the second week in March so that gives us a week to move to Birmingham. Could you find out a few more details about the exact cost and then get back to me?
Thomas I've already started! One of their reps is coming to see me on Thursday.

1 True, False or Don't Know?

1. Grant and Thomas want to decide the promotional budget. ....
2. The Company is exhibiting in Milan. ....
3. PC Times is a new magazine. ....
4. PC Times is very popular. ....
5. The PC Times Show is a new exhibition. ....
6. PC Times is going to advertise in newspapers. ....
7. Grant and Thomas are going to be on TV. ....
8. The PC Times Show is in London. ....
9. The show is on after the show in Milan. ....
10. Thomas has met the rep from the exhibition. ....
11. Grant has decided to exhibit at the PCT Show. ....
12. Thomas is going to get promoted. ....

LANGUAGE STUDY

English has no one future 'tense'. There are different ways to talk about the future.

The **present continuous** is usual to talk about arrangements for the future which were made before now.

I'm meeting him at 6.30. (meeting arranged before now).
(be) going to involves something before now but is also more strongly connected to now.

It's going to rain. (black clouds in the sky before now and now)
With inflation so high, I'm going to ask for an increase in salary.
(you've thought about it earlier but the present situation is part of the decision)

Underline in the dialogue where Thomas and Grant are talking about the future. Decide why they chose to use the **Present Continuous** or **be going to**..

2 Practise saying these with correct stress and intonation.

1. I'm having a party. Would you like to come?
2. He's arriving on the afternoon plane from Paris.
3. I'm stopping over in Singapore.
4. I'm seeing her on Wednesday.
5. It's going to be a nice day.
6. She's going to change her supplier.
7. The Newcastle branch is going to move to bigger premises.
8. They're going to bring out an improved version.

In what situation do you think you might say each sentence?

Set One: Going to

1 Make sentences about the following situations:

1. You want to go to the cinema on Friday. You haven't reserved a ticket.

2. Bill is coming to dinner tomorrow. You want Jane to come but you haven't invited her yet.

3. You are seeing your boss at 10.30. He wants to talk about the problem with the unions.

4. You are going to New York on Tuesday. You plan to visit an old friend who works on Wall Street but you haven't arranged anything.

5. You are starting a new job with I.B.M. in three months time. You plan to tell your boss next month.

2 What is going to happen? Write two sentences for each.

1. Helen doesn't like her present job. She has been offered a new job in a nice company, with a better salary and more responsibility.

2. It is midnight. Malcolm cannot finish his urgent report because there is paper stuck in his photocopier. He has a screwdriver in his office.

3. Louis Michaels is on his plane for Chicago. The last engine has just stopped working. The Atlantic is approaching rapidly.

4. Phil has put in an 'exaggerated' expense claim. His boss wants to see him and she doesn't look very happy.

5. The report was due last week. Brian still hasn't started it.

3 These are Martin's New Year's resolutions. Complete the sentences with the appropriate verb:

ask, meet, get, manage, play

1. I'm going to .... my time better.
2. I'm going to .... more sport.
3. I'm going to .... a new job.
4. I'm going to .... all my deadlines.
5. I'm going to .... for a salary increase.

4 What are your plans for next year?

....

....

....

5 Listening.

Listen to the cassette and choose the best answer.

1. How long is the programme?
    a. 10 minutes
    b. 30 minutes
    c. all night

2. What time does it start?
    a. 9.00
    b. 9.30
    c. 10.00

3. Does Thomas's company make
    a. new computers?
    b. special computers?
    c. power protectors?

4. Has Jean Cooper
    a. just joined Galaxy TV?
    b. just joined the BBC?
    c. never presented a TV programme before?

5. Thomas
    a. is certain to take a stand at the exhibition.
    b. wants more details about the costs.
    c. thinks it is too expensive.

Set Two: Arrangements

1 **You have made the following arrangements. How would you tell a colleague what you have arranged?**

1. You have a ticket for the theatre for next Friday.
   ....

2. You telephoned Bill this morning and invited him for dinner tomorrow evening.
   ....

3. Your boss has just telephoned and has asked you to go to his office at 10.30.
   ....

4. You have a reservation for the Pan Am flight to New York at 11.30 a.m. next Tuesday.
   ....

5. You have accepted a new job with I.B.M. starting in three months time.
   ....

2 **Complete the dialogue using the following verbs:**

attend, have, speak, go, hold,
take, come, spend, fly, stop over

Richard	I hear you .... to Chicago, Alexander.
Alexander	Yes. We .... the GrammaCorp International convention there. It starts on Tuesday so I .... out there on Thursday.
Richard	.... you .... there directly or .... you .... in New York?
Alexander	I .... the direct flight. I'm bored with New York. David .... up from Buffalo and we .... the weekend together in Chicago. David's arranged a great weekend. We .... a cocktail party given by the mayor and then we .... dinner with Jacky Onasser, the millionairess.
Richard	Sounds like a great weekend. What about the conference?
Alexander	Oh these things are always a bit boring. Louis Michaels .... He's one of those eccentric academics, you know.

3 Reading.

THE PC TIMES SHOW

There are many computer shows but this one will be DIFFERENT.

WHERE IS IT?
The Birmingham NEC.
1 hour by train from London (train station on site).
Overhead railway link to
Birmingham International Airport.
Just off the M6 – easy road links to all parts of the UK.

WHEN IS IT?
Thursday 18 October – Sunday 21 October

WHO IS IT FOR?
Thursday and Friday are reserved for the trade. This is a chance for computer professional to sell to computer professional.

WHO'S ORGANIZING IT?
PC Times is part of one of the three largest communications groups in the world. Newspapers, magazines, radio, television all belong to our group. Can you think of a better way to publicize your product?

HOW MUCH DOES IT COST?
Prices start from as low as £65/m^2. See the enclosed booking form and floor plan for details.

HOW TO TAKE PART
Every indication is that space is going to be at a premium for this first exhibition. Please return the enclosed booking form to

PC Times Exhibition,
9 Yarmouth Place
London WC2 8JH

True, False or Don't Know?

1. It is easy to reach the Exhibition Centre. ....
2. You can visit the exhibition on Thursday, 18 October. ....
3. You can only buy on Thursday and Friday. ....
4. They want to find a new way to advertize computers. ....
5. You will pay £65/m^2 for space. ....
6. You need to write to them to get a booking form. ....
7. Walls, carpets and ceilings are provided for the stands. ....
8. There is no space left. ....

Set Three: Vocabulary

1 Find five words which can fill each column in this diagram. Choose words which you think will be useful to you.

Verb	Adjective	
....	....	*visit*
....	....	
....	....	
....	....	
....	....	

2 Complete the chart:

	Verb	Noun
1.	appoint	appointment
2.	dismiss	
3.	resign	
4.		application
5.		employment
6.	promote	
7.		interview
8.		training
9.		production
10.	market	
11.		sales
12.		management

3 Which of these words are concerned with employment (E) and which with computers (C)?

1. database ....
2. overtime ....
3. lay off ....
4. sack ....
5. EDP ....
6. fringe benefits ....
7. promotion ....
8. spreadsheet ....
9. retirement ....
10. word processing ....

Set Four: Vocabulary

1 Which of these verbs could you use with each of the following nouns?

For example, you can postpone a meeting but you cannot *postpone a customer.

postpone, arrange, cancel, make, put off, put back

{ a meeting

{ an appointment

{ a customer

{ a time

PAIR WORK – STUDENT 1

You and your partner are going to run your company's stand at the exhibition. One of you must be there at all times. The exhibition is open from 10.00 am to 8.00 pm on Thursday, Friday, Saturday and Sunday. That is a total of 40 hours and you should aim to work no more than 20 of these each. In addition you plan to visit the stands of some of your competitors. You need at least 5 hours to do this. You have these appointments:

Thursday Meeting at your son's school. Very important you attend (your son is doing badly). You need to leave the exhibition no later than 4.00 pm.

Friday Lunch with a big customer who is visiting the exhibition. You need to be free between 12.00 and 2.00.

Saturday An appointment with your dentist at 9.00. Try not to start before 12.00.

PAIR WORK – STUDENT 2

You and your partner are to run your company's stand at the exhibition. One of you must be there at all times. The exhibition is open from 10.00 am to 8.00 pm on Thursday, Friday, Saturday and Sunday. That is a total of 40 hours and you should aim to work no more than 20 of these each. In addition you plan to visit the stands of some of your competitors. You need at least 5 hours to do this. You have these appointments:

Thursday   Playing golf with the MD. You need to leave at 1.00 but could be back for 6.00.

Friday   Important business meeting in London in the morning. Impossible to postpone. You could be at the exhibition by 3.00.

Saturday   Your cousin is getting married at 4.00. You need to leave at 2.00.

1   It's Your Business.

1. Have you ever run a stand at an exhibition? Did you enjoy it?
2. Are most trade fairs a waste of time?

2   Write.

A promotional letter on behalf of the PC Times Show.

....

....

....

....

STUDY TIP

Don't write complicated English. Keep it simple. Modern written English is clear and direct, especially in business where time is money. If you don't know what to write, first think how you could say the idea in conversation, then write it down – you'll probably only need to make small changes.

Set Five: Using Real Texts

STUDY TIP

This text has not been simplified. Do not try to understand every word. The text is only to help you to learn to read efficiently. It is best if you only do the suggested tasks.

1 **Read the text and decide if the following are True, False, or Don't Know.**

1. A weekly staff meeting must be held at a regular time.
2. It is an opportunity to brainstorm problems.
3. Start with short questions, finish with complex problems.
4. Circulate a report of the meeting to each person.
5. Don't have staff meetings if they are unpopular.
6. Problem-focused meetings must be held regularly.

MEETINGS

Generally speaking, the fewer the better. Both as to the number of meetings and the number of participants.

There are several kinds of useful meetings. Here are a couple:

The Weekly Staff Meeting

Purpose: information, not problem-solving.

Takes place same time same place, like TV news. **Starts on the dot no matter who's missing.**

Goes around the room: reports on problems, developments. (A crossed wire is handled by Joe saying to Pete: "I'll see you after the meeting on that"). A number of people should and will say "Pass."

Ends on the dot (or sooner). No attendance taken. No stigma for non-attendance.

One-page minutes dictated, typed, **and** circulated the same day. Every six months have a secret ballot –" Do we **need** a weekly staff meeting?"

The Problem- (or Opportunity-) Focused Meeting

Shouldn't happen more than a few times a year after a company gets going. A good manager with a nose for when an important problem or opportunity is facing his group earns his salt by calling this meeting. In my experience it's really a series of meetings.

After the first session, some are against, some are for, some think it's all a waste of time. I pick out a well-respected operating man who is reasonably enthusiastic for the idea and pair him with an assistant controller. They come back in a week to report (orally) on whether the idea makes sense.

After this second meeting the idea is either pretty obviously major or you apologize to the group for wasting time.

(from **Up the Organisation** by Robert Townsend)

UNIT 7: Cash Flow

Predictions; Decisions; Offers and promises; Future verb forms.

Listen to the conversation between the owner of a language school and his bank manager and then answer the questions.

Manager Well, Mr Lawson, it's not very good, you know. Your school has been overdrawn for the last six months.
Lawson Yes, but that was in winter. Now that summer is coming, things will be much better. I think that student numbers will be up by 20% and I'm sure we'll be able to clear our overdraft by the middle of next month.
Manager Next month. I see. Could I see your cash flow forecast for the next three months?
Lawson My what?
Manager Your cash flow forecast. I'll explain. You write down the income you think you'll receive – not the sales, just the money you'll get – and then you anticipate your expenses for the same period. Look, take a copy of this booklet. It will explain everything more clearly than I can.
Lawson Thank you very much. I'll read it tonight.
Manager Good, then prepare a forecast. Come back in on Wednesday and we'll talk about it.
Lawson Thank you very much. I'll see you Wednesday.
(outside)
Marston Well, Paul. How did it go?
Lawson Not too bad. I'm going back on Wednesday with a cash flow forecast. She's given me this booklet. I'm going to read it tonight.
Marston Tonight? You can't. You won't have time. You're taking the students to the theatre.
Lawson Oh yes. Silly me. Then I'll stay at home tomorrow morning and read it. Could you look after the office?
Marston Of course, I will.

1 **Answer these questions about the dialogue:**

1. Is the Bank Manager happy with Mr Lawson?
2. Why has the school got an overdraft?
3. What is Mr Lawson's prediction about student numbers?
4. Has Mr Lawson got a cash flow forecast?
5. What does Mr Lawson promise to do?
6. What does the manager promise to do?
7. What is Marston's job?
8. Where do the school's students come from?
9. Why can't Paul Lawson read the booklet tonight?
10. When does he decide to read it?
11. What is the peak month for students?
12. Marston is more efficient than Lawson.

LANGUAGE STUDY

Two important uses of **will** are:

a. When forming an opinion or taking a decision at the moment of speaking (we often use **'ll**).
b. After verbs such as 'hope' 'think' 'estimate' to predict the future. (Be careful! Predictions based on things which are evident now are normally made using **going to**)

Look at the dialogue and underline examples of **will**. Discuss with your teacher why the speaker chose to use **will**.

2 **Read these sentences using correct stress and intonation.**

1. This will be a difficult meeting.
2. I'll do that if you'll phone Head Office.
3. You'll have to use the other copier. This one won't work.
4. She'll never agree.
5. I'll give you three days to find the answer.
6. Don't worry. I'll answer it.
7. Right. I'll get back to you in a couple of days.
8. I'm sure things'll pick up after Christmas.

In what situations do you think you might use each sentence? You may find it useful to learn some of these by heart.

STUDY TIP

Often the differences between the different future forms are very small.
The best way to understand is to look at and listen to lots of examples.
Try to decide why the speaker chose that particular future form.

Set One: Predictions

EXAMPLES
I think that student numbers will be up by 20%.
I'm sure we will be able to clear our overdraft.

1 Say if you agree or disagree with these predictions.

1. I don't think there will ever be a woman President or Prime Minister of my country.
2. I think oil prices will rise next year.
3. I'm sure unemployment will increase next year.
4. I'm certain there will be another nuclear disaster in the next three years.
5. I'm sure there won't be another war in Europe.

2 Complete these dialogues using 'll, will, won't and, where necessary, these verbs:

be, arrive, reach, find, give, say, see, last

1. What time are you coming?
   –Well, I'm leaving my house at ten so I think I .... about 4.00.
2. Do you think you .... agreement?
   –I think we ....
3. I'm certain that our products .... you complete satisfaction.
   –Well, I hope they .... !
4. It's too expensive.
   –Yes, I'm sure we .... something cheaper.
5. Well, I'd better tell the boss we've lost the contract.
   –Yes, he .... very pleased!
6. We're planning to expand into Japan.
   –You .... that an easy market.
7. I hope you .... discrete.
   –Don't worry. I .... a word.
8. This boom .... for ever.
   –Right. I think we .... a fall in sales very soon.

3 Make predictions about:

a. your personal future
promotionmove to new citytravel

b. the future for your company
salesnew productsprofits

c. the future for your country
economypopulationenvironment

4 Listening.

Listen to the radio news and say if these statements are true or false.

1. Germany has announced a record surplus. ....
2. Exports have increased by 25%. ....
3. Imports have decreased by 5%. ....
4. The mark has been revalued. ....
5. This is good for British companies. ....
6. In Italy, inflation is at 5%. ....
7. Interest rates stand at 3%. ....
8. Inflation is likely to increase. ....

This is the analysis of Mr Lawson's sales (in £ '000) for last year by country of origin.
Will Mr Lawson be pleased with or disappointed in today's news?

	June	July	August
Italy	10	10	15
Spain	8	11	15
France	3	2	4
Portugal	3	1	1
Germany	1	1	-
TOTAL	25	25	35

5 Find five words which can fill each column in this diagram. Choose words which you think will be useful to you.

Verb	Adjective	
....	....	
....	....	
....	....	*costs*
....	....	
....	....	

Set Two: Decisions/offers/promises

EXAMPLES
Then I'll stay at home tomorrow morning and read it.
(reaction to news)

I'll read it tonight.

Of course I will.

1 Complete the following using *'ll, will* or *won't*:

1. Could you come and see me this afternoon?
   – Sorry, we have a rush job on. I .... have time.

2. So you'll give me your answer on Friday?
   – Yes, I ....

3. I just don't understand how this spreadsheet works.
   – I .... show you.

4. Can I see last month's sales figures?
   – They're in my office. I .... go and get them.

5. Please remember, this is top secret.
   – Don't worry. I .... tell anyone.

6. Who's going to give the MD the bad news?
   – If no-one else wants to, I ....

2 Complete the sentences using one of these verbs with *'ll*:

see, call back, give, speak, get, answer

1. I feel exhausted.
   – Sit down and I .... you a drink.

2. I've got too much work.
   – I .... you a hand.

3. Until the meeting tomorrow, then.
   – OK, I .... you tomorrow.

4. Bob is being difficult about the meeting.
   – OK, I .... to him.

5. (phone rings)
   I .... it.

6. Can you let me know as soon as possible?
   – OK, I .... you .... tomorrow.

3 Reading.

On the morning of Mr Lawson's return visit to the bank, this article appeared in the Bornton Argus. Read the article and answer these questions.

True, False or Don't Know?

1. There will be an increase in the number of Italian students this year.
2. This will make little difference to the local economy.
3. The "Blue Moon" is going to close.
4. Everyone is optimistic.
5. There will be a lot more German students.

KING LIRA TRAGEDY?

Yesterday's devaluation of the Italian lira was described as a "tragedy for the town" by a Bornton Chamber of Commerce spokesperson. She pointed out that one of Bornton's major sources of income was from foreign students coming for English language training courses. Last year, about 40% of such students came from Italy. These students spent heavily in the town, particularly on the hotels and bed and breakfast accomodation and in pubs, restaurants and night clubs. This year, she estimated, the number of Italian students would drop by between 25% and 50%. A spokesperson for the "Blue Moon" discotheque said that they were very disappointed by the news. He denied that this would put them in financial difficulties but admitted "it won't be one of our best years". Everyone we spoke to was putting on a brave face and hoping that the revaluation of the Deutschmark might encourage more German students to come to Bornton. The Chamber of Commerce spokesperson revealed that they were drawing up plans to increase marketing of Bornton courses in Germany. Let's hope they make their mark there.

Explain the joke in the title.

Explain the joke in the last line.

Set Three: Vocabulary

1 Find five words which can fill each column in this diagram. Choose words which you think will be useful to you.

Verb	Adjective	
......	......	*income*
......	......	
......	......	
......	......	
......	......	

2 Good or bad? What is your opinion of each of these:

1. a boom
2. to grow fast
3. to be your own boss
4. redundancy
5. profits up
6. limited funds
7. sales down
8. a slump
9. promotion
10. sales slacken off

"Business is really terrible – we're supposed to be a tax-loss."

3 Complete these sentences using *'ll* or *won't* with a suitable verb.

1. Our labour costs .... if the unions get their way.
2. Our export income .... unless we find some new markets.
3. We hope Japanese sales .... our export income.
4. Increasing production .... our unit cost.
5. Increasing production .... no effect on our fixed costs.
6. Our margins .... if we increase discounts.

4 What is the difference between these words:

| brochure | leaflet | booklet | report |
| magazine | flier | catalogue | folder |

Set Four: Contrast of Future Forms

1 Look at these pairs of sentences. Which one would be more usual in everyday conversation?

1. a. OK I agree. I'll do it.
   b. OK I agree. I'm going to do it.

2. a. I promised Carol yesterday. I'll speak to him.
   b. I promised Carol yesterday. I'm going to speak to him.

3. a. My mind is made up. I'll buy an Amstrad.
   b. My mind is made up. I'm going to buy an Amstrad.

4. a. No, no, no, I'll pay. You paid last time.
   b. No, no, no, I'm going to pay. You paid last time.

5. a. I've already decided. I'll drive down.
   b. I've already decided. I'm going to drive down.

Remember that if you decide at the moment of speaking, *'ll* is more usual. *(Be) going to* suggests a plan you made earlier.

2 Choose the correct verb form to complete the dialogue:

meet,   attend,   finish,   see,   go,   be,   be

Jane   What appointments have I got for tomorrow?

Secretary   You .... Mr Dunlop at 9.30. Then you .... the meeting with the union reps at 2.00.

Jane   That .... before 5.30. I .... you at 11.00 tomorrow to discuss what to do while I'm on holiday.

Secretary   You .... to Portugal, aren't you?

Jane   Yes, Estoril. I hope the weather .... OK!

Secretary   I'm sure it .... wonderful.

PAIR WORK – STUDENT 1

You are the Bank Manager. Mr Lawson has prepared his cash flow forecast. See if his predictions about income are reasonable, remembering the bad news about Italian students, and find out if there are any areas where he could cut costs.

PAIR WORK – STUDENT 2

You are Mr Lawson. Your cash flow forecast is set out below. Make a convincing presentation of this to your Bank Manager.

(£'000)

	June	July	August
B/f	−10	−5	0
Income (note 1)	25	25	35
Expenditure	−20	−20	−20
C/f	−5	0	15

Note 1 Almost all students pay at the start of their courses. You have predicted that there will be enough extra German students to balance the loss of Italian students.

Your total costs per month are made up of:

Your salary	£ 3,500
10 teachers' salary	£ 10,100
2 admin. salaries	£ 2,400
Books and material	£ 500
Photocopies	£ 1,300
Rent	£ 1,200
Interest + Miscellaneous	£ 1,000
Total	£ 20,000

1 It's your business.

1. How does your company control liquidity?
2. What training should be given to small businessmen?

2 Write.

A letter from the bank to Mr Lawson confirming what you decided in the meeting.

STUDY TIP

Most students of English can correct many of their mistakes in writing without help. Check your text for simple errors : the most common are "s" at the end of a word, singular noun with plural verb or vice versa, and word order – subject, verb, object.
Finished? Now check again!

Set Five: Using Real Texts

1   What is the main message of this text?

a. Don't develop ideas without evaluation.
b. Don't waste time on impossible ideas.
c. Lateral thinking is a logical process.
d. Don't stop unusual ideas developing.
e. Lateral thinking can make us look foolish.

> ### Delaying Judgement
>
> Your aim in creative thinking should be to separate the evaluation of ideas from their generation. The worst mistake you can make is to kill off new ideas too quickly. It is always easy to find ten ways of saying "no" to anything. For example:
>
> - It won't work
> - We're already doing it
> - It's been tried before without success
> - It's not practical
> - It won't solve the problem
> - It's too risky
> - It's based on pure theory
> - It will cost too much
> - It will antagonize the customers/the boss/the union/the workers/the shareholders, etc.
> - It will create more problems than it solves.
>
> Some of these objections may be valid. But they should be held back until you have generated as many ideas as possible. Allow ideas to grow a little. Don't strangle them at birth.
>
> It is too easy to say "no", too easy to ridicule anything new or different. In creative thinking it is the end result that counts, and if you want it to be original you must not worry too much about the route you follow to get there. It doesn't matter if you stumble sometimes or take the wrong turning, as long as delays are not protracted and you arrive in the right place at the end.
>
> As de Bono says:
>
>> *In vertical thinking one has to be right at every step. So, no matter how many steps are taken, the end point (idea, solution, conclusion) is automatically right if all the intervening steps have been right .... In lateral thinking one does not **have** to be right at each step, but one must be right at the **end**.*
>
> Delaying judgement is difficult. It goes against the grain. You have to make a conscious effort to hold back until the right moment arrives, which is when you feel that you have collected as many new ideas as you can in the time available.

(from **How to be a Better Manager** by Michael Armstrong)

UNIT 8: Fenton

Tags and closing questions;
Vocabulary; Prepositions.

Fenton		I'm sorry Mr Smith but you are wasting your time. We are quite satisfied with our present supplier of silicon widgets.
Smith		I see. But you agree it is a good idea to make comparisons from time to time, don't you?
Fenton		Well yes.
Smith		And you'd be interested in a silicon widget that offered savings of up to 22%, wouldn't you?
Fenton		Of course.
Smith		And you've seen the excellent reports in the trade press, haven't you?
Fenton		Yes, of course.
Smith		And you're going to need silicon widgets with a greater tolerance of high temperatures, aren't you?
Fenton		Certainly.
Smith		So if I could offer you high quality silicon widgets with better resistance to high temperatures for less than you pay for your present widgets, you wouldn't turn down the chance to try them out at a special introductory price, would you?
Fenton		No, of course not. What exactly are you proposing?
Smith		Well ....

1 True or False?

1. At first, Fenton wants to buy from Smith.
2. Smith persuades Fenton to try his widgets.
3. Smith's widgets are better.
4. There have been good reports on the widgets in the press.
5. The new widgets are more flexible than the old ones.

2 Complete these using word partnerships from the dialogue.

1. He's interested ………… the widget.
2. He didn't want the job so he turned it ……………… .
3. He wanted to test the widget so he tried it ………… for a few days.
4. Airmail gives a saving ………… at least three days.
5. I'm not very satisfied ………… such a low discount.

LANGUAGE STUDY

Tags are very important for anyone who has to sell an idea or a product. They encourage the other person to have the same opinion as the speaker (often called a 'closing' question).
Do you like the colour? (Equal chance of 'Yes'/'No' answers)
The colour's nice, isn't it? (Encourages the answer 'Yes').
Underline the examples of 'closing' questions in the dialogue.
Notice that the auxiliary is repeated in the tag.
Positive sentences have negative tags and negative sentences have positive tags.

3 Practise saying them with correct stress and intonation.

1. It's a very compact model, isn't it?
2. They're much more reliable than they were, aren't they?
3. They've become much quieter, haven't they?
4. The taste's improved, hasn't it?
5. They won't change these for years now, will they?
6. They can't make it any smaller, can they?
7. You could sell thousands of these, couldn't you?
8. Your customers will love these, won't they?

Can you think of a product which each of these sentences might be describing?

STUDY TIP

Every word which begins with a vowel sound is linked to the word before it. For example, the last part of "Can't you ?" is pronounced almost like the word 'chew'.
Remember to join the words together when you learn a useful expression.

Set One: Tags

1 Turn these into 'closing' questions:

1. This is the best solution, ...
2. You're going to need a second supplier, ...
3. Murphy's the best candidate, ...
4. We've got the answer, ...
5. You haven't found the perfect answer yet, ...
6. You're not going to do that, ...
7. You could sell more in Scotland, ...
8. You can see the advantages, ...
9. You would be interested in a higher quality product at the same price, ...
10. You wouldn't have any trouble selling these, ...

LANGUAGE STUDY

The tag for **will** is **won't**, for example **You'll let me know, won't you?**
If there is no auxiliary in the main sentence, use **don't, doesn't, didn't** in the tag, for example **You see the advantages, don't you? You sold out of the K49 very quickly, didn't you?**

2 Turn these into 'closing' questions:

1. You need the latest technology, ...
2. It won't work, ...
3. It'll never be a success, ...
4. You don't want to be stuck with outdated technology, ...
5. Munich didn't reach their target, ...
6. Your investment paid off last time, ...
7. It'll be a disaster, ...
8. Your company insists on the best quality, ...
9. The Chairman told us to get the best solution regardless of cost, ...
10. You wouldn't like me to raise this with the boss, ...
11. It costs less than you'd expect, ...
12. It looks very neat, ...

3 What closing questions could you use:

a. to get a salary increase.
b. to get a job in the New York office.
c. to get your boss to do more work and delegate less to you.

4 Listen to these tags:

These sentences are recorded twice. The first time they are questions for information (the tag rises). The second time they are closing questions (the tag falls).

1. It's quicker to fly, isn't it?
2. You're happy with that, aren't you?
3. You got the order, didn't you?
4. The end of July will be early enough, won't it?
5. He wants to buy an Italian machine, doesn't he?
6. They're going to order, aren't they?

Now listen again. This time the questions are sometimes for information (I) and sometimes are closing questions (C). Identify which.

Write your answers here:

1	2	3	4	5	6

Ask your teacher the questions and check that your intonation is correct.

5 Find five words which can fill each column in this diagram. Choose words which you think will be useful to you.

Verb	Adjective	
....	....	*sales*
....	....	
....	....	
....	....	
....	....	

6 Listening.

Freddy Fenton of Purchasing is talking to Harry Harris of Production. Listen and answer the questions.

1. How many of the new silicon widgets has Fenton ordered?
2. When is Harris going to test them?
3. When will he give Fenton his report?

Set Two: Tags and Vocabulary

1 Match the response to the tag statements:

1. You can use a word-processor, can't you?
2. You're not going to accept their offer, are you?
3. Michael worked in Home Sales for a while, didn't he?
4. They aren't the best on the market, are they?
5. You've met him, haven't you?
6. You agree with that, don't you?

a. Yes, just before he went off to Japan.
b. Yes, I went on a course last year.
c. Well actually, in my opinion they are.
d. No, but I know him by reputation.
e. What else can I do?
f. Up to a point, yes.

Write your answers here:

1	2	3	4	5	6

LANGUAGE STUDY

Tags are often used to direct a conversation. They often invite the other person to agree, and to make a further comment. You can see this in the examples above.

2 Ask the other person to comment or confirm what you think.

1. You're Harry,............................?
2. You don't approve of this decision,............................?
3. Donald's flying in tomorrow,............................?
4. Tax forms have to be sent in by 31st March,............................?
5. You two have already met,............................?
6. Head office agreed,............................?
7. You've had this problem before,............................?
8. You're going to help me,............................?
9. They must like you in Head Office,............................?

STUDY TIP

The rules for forming these are very simple and mechanical. However, most students have a lot of problems using question tags in ordinary conversation. You need to practise quite a lot.
Make yourself a cassette of these exercises without the tags and leaving spaces between the examples. Practise saying them in the car, adding the tags.

3 Reading.

MEMO

Freddy,

We have tested the new silicon widgets from Smith. They are certainly much more heat resistant. I estimate that on average we can get 10% extra use from these compared to our existing widgets. That would mean that we would need about 5000 a month. As you know, we have 2 months stock of the old widgets in the warehouse at present. I would be happy to change over once these have been used up, provided the cost doesn't go up.

Harry

True or False?

1. Harris likes the new widgets.
2. The new widgets are technically better.
3. The new widgets are 10% bigger.
4. Harris uses about 5500 of the present widgets per month.
5. There are 10000 widgets in stock.
6. Harris insists upon changing.

4 Match the verb to the noun:

1. raise
2. take
3. make
4. invest in
5. lose
6. close

a. a fortune
b. prices
c. a factory
d. a contract
e. risks
f. a project

Write your answers here:

1	2	3	4	5	6

5 The same or different?

1. salesman — representative
2. worker — employee
3. subsidiary — branch
4. enter a market — break into a market
5. England — Britain
6. politics — policies
7. I'd rather — I'd prefer
8. overseas — abroad
9. stock (UK) — inventory (US)
10. stock (US) — share (UK)

Set Three: Auxiliaries

EXAMPLE

Did you go to the meeting yesterday?
 –No.
 –No I didn't.

The second answer is much friendlier than the first and helps to keep the conversation going.

1 Give similar short answers to these questions:

1. Have you ever worked for an American company?
   No, ...
2. Did you learn a lot at Business School?
   No, ...
3. Is English important for your job?
   Yes, ...
4. Do you work hard?
   Yes, ...
5. Will they be finished by Tuesday?
   No, ...
6. Does Dorothy know about the meeting?
   Yes, ...

LANGUAGE STUDY

Remember, we have already noticed that tags often invite an extra comment, new information which develops the conversation. These examples are similar. The most natural answers involve answering and giving a new comment.

2 Do the last exercise again and try to add an extra comment each time.

LANGUAGE STUDY

If you want to give an interested response to someone, repeat the first auxiliary. (use **do/does/did** if there is no auxiliary)

3 Give interested responses to these statements:

1. IBM have just announced price cuts.
   Oh, ...
2. I met Mario at the Milan Trade Fair last week.
   Oh, ...
3. I'm going to Geneva next week.
   Oh, ...
4. I was in Zurich last week.
   Oh,..
5. I've already discussed that with them.
   Oh, ...
6. The boss wants to see you.
   Oh, ...

Set Four: Prepositions

1 **Put in one of the following:**

at,   in,   on,   to,   of,   with,   over

1. I'm not very good .... English.
2. Have you heard .... Bjorn Bergman?
3. Are you interested .... joining us?
4. I need to think it ....
5. We're very proud .... our new water-pump.
6. I've been working .... my report.
7. I'm enjoying working .... Michael.
8. We're moving .... Hong Kong.
9. I'm looking .... different possibilities.
10. He's happy .... what you have done.

2 **Put in one of the following if necessary:**

at,   in,   on,   until,   from,   to

1. I start work .... 8.30.
2. I usually have lunch .... 12.30 .... 1.15.
3. I work .... I'm finished!
4. I'm arriving .... Tuesday.
5. I'm arriving .... March.
6. I'm arriving .... March 22nd.
7. I'm staying .... Tuesday .... Friday.
8. I'm arriving .... tomorrow.
9. Barbara started working in Singapore .... 1989.
10. Meet me .... 10.00 am .... Tuesday, 22nd March.

PAIR WORK — STUDENT 1

You are Freddy Fenton. You are prepared to buy silicon widgets from Andrew Smith, provided the terms are right.

Your present terms are:

5500 widgets per month at £70 per hundred (£3850 p.m.)

Payment at 30 days.

If you can get similar terms from Smith, do a deal.

Remember that you only need 5000 of Smith's widgets so you can afford to pay up to £77 per hundred.

PAIR WORK — STUDENT 2

You are Andrew Smith.
Your list price per hundred for quantities between 4000 and 6000 widgets per month is £850 per thousand.
Your company authorises you to offer reductions of up to 20% (i.e. £170 per thousand). Your bonus is calculated upon the difference between list price and the price your client pays.
Payment is at 60 days and there is a reduction of £30 per thousand for payment within 30 days. Close the sale!

1 It's Your Business.

What's the best way to sell products or ideas in your country? Do you prefer potential suppliers to give you the hard sell or the soft sell? Have you tried using these techniques with people of other nationalities? Were they successful?

2 Writing.

Write a memo about your discussion.

Set Five: Using Real Texts

STUDY TIP

With a difficult text such as the one opposite, don't 'block' on individual words. Try to get the general sense of the text : the questions will help you to do this. Once you have understood the general sense, you will probably find that you can guess the meaning of some words and expressions you don't know.

1 Read the text in 3 minutes and answer these questions:

1. What job did the author do?
   a. He was regional sales manager for Ford.
   b. He sold eggs.
2. Ford wanted to promote
   a. safety.
   b. eggs.
3. The dashboard had crash padding so that
   a. people would want to hit their heads on it.
   b. people would buy the car because it was safer.
4. The author wanted
   a. to throw eggs.
   b. to sell the idea of safety better than in the film.

5. The first two eggs
   a. landed on the padding and broke.
   b. did not land on the padding.
6. The third and fourth eggs
   a. landed on the padding and broke.
   b. landed on the padding and did not break.
7. The fifth egg
   a. landed on the padding and broke.
   b. landed on the padding and did not break.
8. The audience
   a. thought it was very funny.
   b. was impressed by the demonstration.
9. The main lesson to be learnt is
   a. Eggs help you to sell.
   b. Practise what you are going to say/do before you do it.

> When it rains, it pours, and for me it rained pretty hard in 1956. That was the year Ford decided to promote auto safety rather than performance and horsepower. The company introduced a safety package that included crash padding for the dashboard. The factory had sent along a film for us to show the dealers, which was supposed to explain just how much safer the new padding was in the event that a passenger hit his head on the dash. To illustrate the point, the narrator in the film claimed the padding was so thick that if you dropped an egg on it from a two-storey building, the egg would bounce right off without breaking.
>
> I was hooked. Instead of having the salesmen learn about the safety padding from the film, I would make the point far more dramatically by actually dropping an egg onto the padding. About eleven hundred men sat in the audience at the regional sales meeting as I began to make my pitch about the terrific new safety padding we were offering in our 1956 models. I had spread strips of padding across the stage, and now I climbed on a high ladder with a carton of fresh eggs.
>
> The very first egg I dropped missed the padding altogether and splattered on the wooden floor. The audience roared with delight. I took more careful aim with the second egg, but my assistant, who was holding the ladder, chose this moment to move in the wrong direction. As a result, the egg bounced off his shoulder. This, too, was greeted with wild applause.
>
> The third and fourth eggs landed exactly where they were supposed to. Unfortunately, they broke on impact. Finally, with the fifth egg, I achieved the desired result – and got a standing ovation. I learned two lessons that day. First, never use eggs at a sales rally. And second, never go before your customers without rehearsing what you want to say – as well as what you're going to do – to help sell your product.

(from **Iacocca, an autobiography** by Lee Iacocca)

UNIT 9: Sophia Antipolis
Checking and Correcting Information;
Confirming with tags; Two-word expressions.

Agent	Brooklyn Travel. Can I help you?
Secretary	Good morning. This is Whiterock Systems. I'd like to make some travel arrangements for my boss.
Agent	Certainly. What's his name?
Secretary	**Her** name is Tait, Mrs Stephanie Tait.
Agent	It's a bad line. Could you repeat that, please?
Secretary	Tait. Stephanie Tait.
Agent	Tait?
Secretary	Yes, that's right.
Agent	Is that T-A-T-E?
Secretary	No. T-A-I-T.
Agent	OK. What exactly does Mrs Tait require?
Secretary	She has to visit several companies in Sophia Antipolis.
Agent	Sophia ....?
Secretary	Antipolis.
Agent	Could you spell that please?
Secretary	It's two words. S-O-P-H-I-A new word A-N-T-I-P-O-L-I-S.
Agent	And that's in Greece?
Secretary	Not Greece, France. It's near Antibes.
Agent	Oh yes, of course. That's the 'French Silicon Valley', isn't it?
Secretary	Yes. Mrs Tait needs to go there from the 8th to the 12th of next month. So she'll need the flight, business class, a hotel and a car.
Agent	So an early flight to Nice on the 8th, a hire car, four nights in a hotel near Sophia Antipolis and a return flight on the afternoon of the 12th?
Secretary	That's right.
Agent	You said business class, didn't you?
Secretary	Yes.
Agent	OK. I'll get on to that straightaway. I'll phone you back within the hour.
Secretary	Fine. Thank you.

1 Answer the questions:

1. Who does the secretary work for?
2. Why doesn't the travel agent understand the name?
3. Where does Mrs Tait want to go?
4. When does Mrs Tait want to go?
5. What does the travel agent have to arrange?

LANGUAGE STUDY
Underline in the dialogue

- 4 ways of getting the speaker to repeat or confirm what they have said.
- 2 ways of checking that the other person has understood correctly.
- 1 way of correcting the other person when they have **not** understood correctly.

2 Find five words which can fill each column in this diagram. Choose words which you think will be useful to you.

Verb	Adjective	
		arrangement

3 Practise saying these with the correct stress and intonation:

1. It's a bad line. Could you repeat your name, please?
2. I can't hear you very well. Could you repeat that, please?
3. Harry Roberts from ....?
4. You're arriving on the ....?
5. Thursday?
6. £250?
7. Can I call you back in a few minutes?
8. You're arriving on Thursday, aren't you?

In what situation do you think you might say each one?

STUDY TIP
Don't be afraid to exaggerate your intonation. English intonation goes up and down much more than many languages. Listen to the "music" when English people speak – try to reproduce the same "music".

Set One: Checking and Correcting Information

EXAMPLE
She has to visit several companies in Sophia Antipolis.
– Sophia ………?
– Antipolis.

---

1 Work in pairs.

xxxxx represents the part one person doesn't hear or understand completely. That person asks for a repeat. The other person should give the correct information as clearly as possible.

1. My name is Margaret Thxxxxx.   (Thurlow)
2. We will deliver on xxxxxsday.   (Thursday)
3. The XXY costs twenty-xxxxx pounds each. (£23)
4. This is my colleague, James Txxxxx.   (Thatcher)
5. My name's Rupert Fxxxxx.   (Fox)
6. We must have the parts by mid -xxxxxber. (October)

EXAMPLES
And that's in Greece?
– Not Greece, France.

---

2 Correct these misunderstandings:

1. My name is Thatcher.
   Hello Mr. Thitter.
2. The price is £50.
   £15?
3. Let's meet again in July.
   OK. What date in June?
4. The price includes VAT.
   So that's exclusive of VAT.
5. We're meeting on the 13th.
   Friday the 14th.
6. We've put you into the Hotel Princess.
   The Hotel Prince – is that the one in the square?
7. Their quantity control is very bad.
   We have no trouble with their quality?
8. I've just got back from a trip to Switzerland.
   How was Stockholm?

What is the difference between a **journey** and a **trip**?
Remember that the word **voyage** is very unusual. It is used for a long sea journey but now almost only for cargo.

EXAMPLE
You said business class, didn't you?

3 Check you have understood correctly.

1. My name is Neil.
2. I come from Bilbao.
3. That costs 20,000 pesetas.
4. We've booked you a room at the Hotel du Lac.
5. Can I come and see you on Thursday?
6. We'd like to order 20 kilos.

4 Which of the following things do you usually take with you on a trip abroad?

a. if it's a business trip?
b. if it's a pleasure trip?

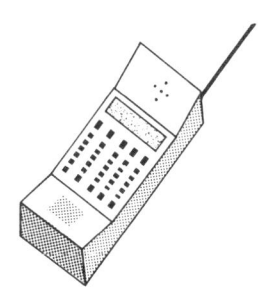

a credit card
a mobile phone
a calculator

your diary
swimming things
a calendar

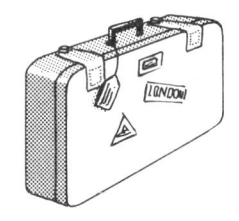

a portable PC
your briefcase
a suitcase

Why is it easier to fly if you have a briefcase not a suitcase?

5 Listening.

The travel agent found out the necessary information and phoned the secretary back. Listen to their conversation and answer these questions.
1. What's the problem with the seven thirty and ten o'clock flights?
2. What's the problem with the twelve fifteen flight?
3. What alternative does the travel agent propose?
4. What does the secretary decide?
5. What car does the agent suggest?

Set Two: Confirming with Tags

EXAMPLE
That's the 'French Silicon Valley', isn't it?

1 Add the correct tag to the following:

1. You're Frank, ...?
2. You're coming to the meeting, ...?
3. You're going to come, ...?
4. You've been here before, ...?
5. You'll do it, ...?
6. It's feasible, ...?

2 Add the correct tag to the following:

1. They're not very easy to deal with, ...?
2. You're not leaving the company, ...?
3. The unions are not going to like it, ...?
4. You haven't seen our new model yet, ...?
5. They won't agree to that, ...?
6. It isn't what we want, ...?

3 Add the correct tag to the following:

1. You work for IBM, ...?
2. You went to the last meeting, ...?
3. He speaks enough Italian to handle the job, ...?
4. You don't like him, ...?
5. You didn't accept those terms, ...?
6. She doesn't like travelling, ...?

4 Complete the dialogue with appropriate tags.

Nick	Now, Jeremy, you promised us delivery last Tuesday, ...?
Jeremy	Yes, I did.
Nick	And your company knew we had almost none left in stock, ...?
Jeremy	Yes, we did.
Nick	But you didn't deliver any, ...?
Jeremy	No, we didn't.
Nick	So my factory has had to stop production, ...?
Jeremy	Yes, I'm sorry.
Nick	Sorry! That's not a lot of help, ..., Jeremy?

5 Reading.

On the last day of her visit to Sophia Antipolis, Mrs Tait received this fax from her secretary.

FAX

Mrs Tait,

I had an urgent phone call from Jose Ruiz. It appears that the control system we installed in his water treatment unit is not working correctly. He is very worried about the potential pollution problem and asks you to come and see him immediately. I told him you were tied up today but could probably arrange to fly to Barcelona tomorrow. I assume you will do this and I have rearranged your appointments here for tomorrow. Hope this is correct.

Everything here is under control.

I imagine you look suntanned after four days in the South of France!

Enjoy your trip to Barcelona.

Susan
Susan

True, False or Don't Know?

1. Mrs Tait is in France.
2. Mrs Tait has worked hard.
3. Jose Ruiz has got an urgent problem.
4. Mrs Tait has got a ticket to Barcelona.
5. Mrs Tait has a lot of appointments tomorrow.
6. There are no problems in England.
7. Mrs Tait has been lying in the sun.
8. The secretary thinks that travelling to other countries on business is tiring and boring.

Set Three: Two Word Expressions

1 Put one word into each space:

We wanted to break .... the EC so we decided to set .... a subsidiary in an EC country. We looked .... several countries before deciding .... the UK. Our decision was based .... different factors; the amount .... government grants, the quality and quantity .... skilled labour and the choice .... sites. We also wanted to be close .... our biggest customers. .... the end, we took .... an English competitor which had run .... liquidity problems because of the rise .... the dollar.

2 Add one word in each space. Then underline all the two-word verbs that are made with the verb (*get*).

When I got .... the plane, the first person I saw was Bill Hardcastle. Bill was no longer young: in fact he was getting .... a bit. We had a good relationship, we got .... really well and I knew that, if I had a major problem, all I had to do was get .... to him and he would help me get .... it. We started talking about work but soon got .... the subject. He told me that he had got .... at 3.00 that morning to make an important telephone call to Japan but that he hadn't been able to get .... He had got .... the operator but she had been very rude. He had become angry, had got .... a temper and shouted and she had told him to get lost. He still hadn't got .... it.

"Everything I turned my hand to was a disaster until I got into running Business Management Courses."

Set Four: Vocabulary

1 Give the adjective for each of these countries:

1. France   *French*
2. Britain   ....
3. Germany   ....
4. Denmark   ....
5. Greece   ....
6. Italy   ....
7. Portugal   ....
8. Spain   ....
9. Holland   ....
10. Ireland   ....

What other countries are members of the EC?
Which other countries do you often do business with?
Write the countries and their adjectives here.

....

....

2 Look at this sentence:

I'll catch the early train.

How many words or expressions can you find which can replace:

a. catch
b. early
c. train

You can change the meaning of the sentence but you must keep the idea of travelling, so, for example, you could make this sentence:

> **I'll get the last possible flight.**

PAIR WORK – STUDENT 1

You are Mrs Tait. You are in a travel agent's in Nice. You need to get to Barcelona as quickly as possible.

PAIR WORK – STUDENT 2

You are a travel agent in Nice in the South of France. Help Mrs Tait.

Possible methods of travel are:

Plane

Depart	Arrive	
9.30	10.30	(Tomorrow full)
16.30	17.30	(Too late for today, tomorrow OK)

Train

Depart	Arrive	
6.00	12.30	(No problems for tomorrow)
23.30	6.20	(No couchettes or wagon-lits available)

Car

Can rent in Nice and leave in Barcelona. Takes about eight hours but, since this is a holiday period, there may be traffic jams on the French motorways and long queues at the border.

---

1 It's Your Business.

1. How often do you visit different countries in your job?
2. Do you enjoy business trips? What are your best and worst experiences of business travel?

2 Write.

Write the fax that Mrs Tait sends to her secretary informing her of her plans.

Set Five: Using Real Texts

1 **What is the main message of this text:**

a. Schools teach people to exercise.
b. You need to take exercise to be a good manager.
c. People who work hard get lots of exercise.

Read for only 3 minutes. Do not worry about what you **don't** understand. Look for language you **do** understand.

> **Exercise**
>
> Three workouts a week, every other day, is what it takes to keep your body fit enough so that your emotions and your body won't be a drag on your mind. Even people with physically demanding jobs usually need a well-rounded exercise programme. Why? Because almost all workercise is repetitive; a few muscles and joints get all the exercise; the other parts of the body get very little. Funercise is different. Swimming, jogging, playing ball, walking – all these activities benefit the entire body.
>
> Why aren't you exercising regularly now? Thousands of young people develop an enduring hatred for all forms of physical activity in physical education classes. What they learn there is physical de-education.
>
> Maybe you think you can't find the time for exercise. The truth is that you can't afford not to take the time. A well-designed and regularly repeated exercise programme will improve the quality of your sleep and increase your alertness. It will vastly improve your attitude. It will help calm your fears, help keep your difficulties in perspective, and help keep depression away. By doing all these things, a regular and sensible exercise programme will raise the quality of your decisions and multiply your productivity.

(from **The Official Guide to Success** by Tom Hopkins)

Workercise and **funercise** are invented words. What do you think they mean?

Is exercise important for a manager?

UNIT 10: Commodities

Describing graphs; Prepositions of time; Business Game.

Listen to this conversation between a currency dealer and another banker and answer the questions.

Terry Good morning Rob. You're here early. It's only just turned eight o'clock.
Rob Yes, I came in early because of Tokyo. There's been a lot of trading in currencies during the night. I was following on my bleeper and I didn't get much sleep. So I came in early.
Terry What's happened?
Rob Well in early trading, the dollar fell sharply against the Swiss franc and slightly against the European snake. But it rose against the yen.
Terry How do you explain that?
Rob Well, the price of petrol is rising quickly because of the problems in the Gulf. And the dollar is a bit weak because of the President's health problems. And the yen went down because Japanese exports are decreasing.
Terry What do you think will happen this morning?
Rob Well I think there will be some profit taking. Probably, the dollar will recover and go back up a bit against the Swiss franc. But I think the yen will continue to go down.
Terry What about the snake?
Rob It may go up or down! It's difficult to say.

1 Answer these questions about the dialogue. Sometimes you may not find the information you need in the dialogue.

1. Why did Rob get so little sleep?
2. What do you think a 'bleeper' is?
3. When did Rob visit Tokyo?
4. What has happened to the dollar? Why?
5. What has happened to the mark? Why?
6. What has happened to the Swiss franc? Why?
7. What has happened to the yen? Why?
8. What does Rob think will happen?

LANGUAGE STUDY

Very often in business, we want to talk about changes. We often present information about changes on graphs, so most business people need the language to describe graphs.

2 Divide the following words into two groups, one showing an increase, the other a decrease.

Use two marker pens, one for positive words and one for negative words.

rise	slide	plummet	recover
collapse	dip	grow	come down
rocket	fall	drop	slump
weaken	soar	dive	stage a comeback
jump	improve	deteriorate	rebound

3 Translate these into your own language:

You can be much clearer if you can also say how something changed. Here are the most important words for this. Make sure you understand them all.

sharply	slowly	steadily ....
steeply	slightly	suddenly ....
dramatically	immediately	gradually ....

4 Give examples from your own situation of something which has done these things recently:

1. fallen steadily ....
2. increased dramatically ....
3. rocketed suddenly ....
4. dipped sharply ....
5. recovered gradually ....
6. collapsed totally ....

Set One: Describing Graphs

1 Match the sentence to the graph.

1. The price peaked at $2.37.
2. The price levelled off at $2.37.
3. The price stands at $2.37.
4. The price bottomed out around $2.37.

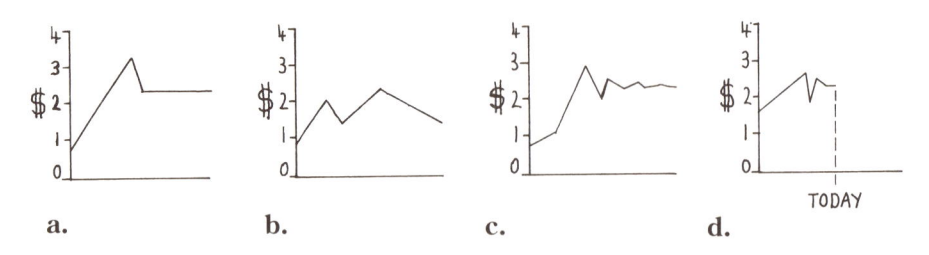

a.   b.   c.   d.

Use these words to label the same graphs.

reach high of   reach a low of

EXAMPLES

Notice the prepositions in these expressions:
The price fell by 25% from $2.62 to $2.37.
Between noon and close of trading, the Dow Jones fell by more than 25 points.

Notice the verbs in these expressions:
European sales increased by 12% last year.
Oil prices have risen by 10% in the last three months.
The dollar is rising steadily against the Swiss franc at the moment.
Commodity prices will probably increase by 20% before the end of the year.

2 Now draw three simple graphs to show:

1. how your salary has changed since you left school or college.
2. your energy level from 6.00 yesterday to eleven o'clock yesterday evening.
3. some change you are familiar with in your work situation.

3 Now describe the graphs you have drawn.

If you use a lot of graphs in your work, find some useful ones and make sure you can describe them in words.

4 Listening.

Listen to the description of the rise and fall of the dollar against the dotte and complete the chart.

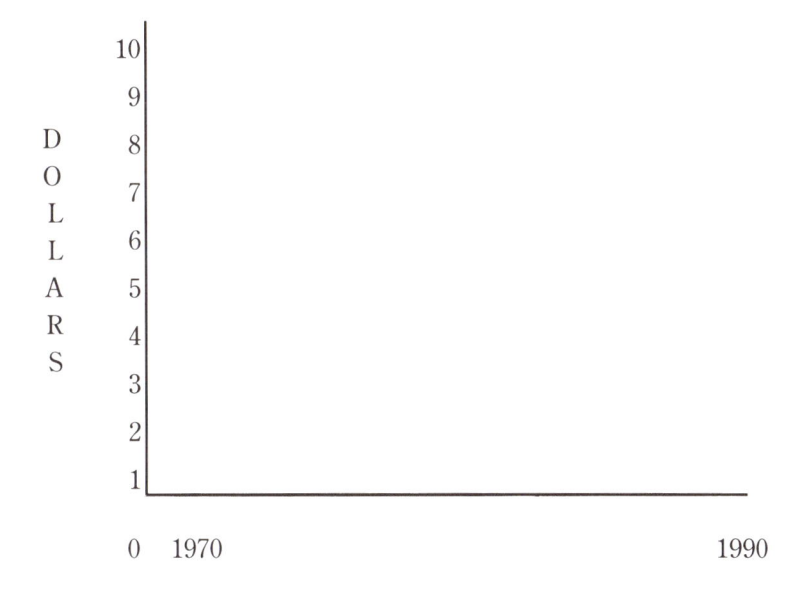

```
       10
        9
D       8
O       7
L
L       6
A       5
R
S       4
        3
        2
        1
        0   1970                              1990
```

5 Listen to the description of the number of units produced week by week and complete the chart.

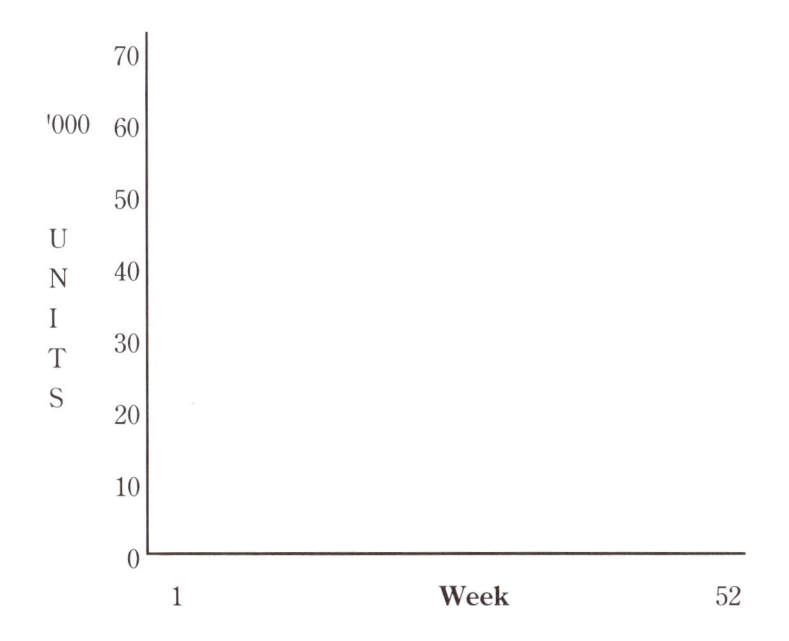

```
        70
'000    60
        50
U
N       40
I
T       30
S
        20
        10
         0
             1              Week              52
```

Set Two: Prepositions of Time

LANGUAGE STUDY

We often use time expressions when we are talking about changes. Look at the text of the listening (page 156) and underline the time expressions used by the speakers.

1 Match up these three prepositions with the phrases:

a. on   **b.** in   **c.** at

1. 1992
2. Friday
3. the weekend
4. June
5. the second of June
6. two o'clock
7. lunchtime
8. Christmas
9. the morning
10. the moment
11. the next century
12. the end of the week

1	2	3	4	5	6	7	8	9	10	11	12

2 Complete these sentences using one of these prepositions:

for   since   over   during

Sometimes more than one is possible.
1. We've had a lot of labour problems .... the last few months.
2. Productivity was surprisingly good .... the summer.
3. We've had a lot less problems .... we changed supplier.
4. Prices have risen sharply .... the last few months.
5. I'm sure they'll continue to rise .... some time.
6. Profits have fallen by 20% .... Mark left the company.
7. The market has doubled .... the last year.
8. The pound stood at $ 2.40 .... several years.

3 Write some sentences about you or your company using:

over   since   during   for

....

....

....

....

4 Reading.

Read this newspaper article. Use highlighter pens to mark the time expressions and the expressions of increase or decrease.

LATEST TRADE FIGURES

Britain's current-account stood at £1.12 billion in December, 1989. This was its lowest for 15 months and the fifth consecutive monthly decline. The total deficit for the year was £20.31 billion, up from £14.67 billion in 1988. Exports and imports grew at similar rates during 1989; exports by 10% and imports by 9.5%. However, export growth picked up strongly over the last quarter of the year while imports slowed. The volume of exports in the fourth quarter was 15% up on a year ago while import volumes rose by only 3.5%.

Britain's North Sea oil surplus, which was affected by accidents and shutdowns, recovered by the end of the year. The surplus in the final quarter was £529m. Overall, the oil surplus was £1.4 billion. This is only half the surplus of 2.8 billion in 1988.

5 True, False or Don't Know?

1. Britain's current-account improved during 1989. ....
2. December 1989 was a very bad month. ....
3. The deficit was more in 1989 than in 1988. ....
4. Exports grew more than imports during 1989. ....
5. Car imports fell. ....
6. Exports in the fourth quarter were higher than in 1988. ....
7. Imports in the fourth quarter were higher than in 1988. ....
8. The future is very promising. ....
9. There were problems in North Sea oil production. ....
10. The North Sea result is better than that of 1988. ....

Set Three: Revision

1 Present perfect or past simple ? Choose the correct verb form :

Valex has been founded / was founded in 1975. Since that time it has become / became the leader in its field. Its results have been / were particularly spectacular since it has merged / merged with a German company. Turnover increased/has increased by 200% between 1980 and 1985. The company continued/has continued to expand steadily but less spectacularly. For example, in 1989, sales increased/have increased by 15%

Valex has been / was one of the first consultants to introduce a fully integrated range of communications training courses onto the European Market. Since it has begun / began training for multinational corporations in 1978, Valex has trained / trained over ten thousand people, many of whom have returned / returned for refresher courses every two or three years.

Corporate profits have reached / reached record levels last year, and further expansion is expected. In 1988 the Board has taken / took the decision to go public : in view of the stock market crash which followed, however, this step has been postponed / was postponed for the time being.

*"Good Heavens, Adkins! Didn't they teach you **anything** at the Harvard Business School?"*

2 Find five words which can fill each column in this diagram. Choose words which you think will be useful to you.

Adjective		Verb
....	*prices have*	....
....		....
....		....
....		....
....		....

BUSINESS GAME

This game can be played by 2 or more players. You need two dice and some paper.

Each player starts the game with £1000. Your job is to buy and sell commodities. After 10 turns, the winner is the person with the most money.

There are 3 commodities:

Rubber   low risk
Chocolate some risk
Tin   high risk

All commodities start off at £100 a unit. Investors can buy as many units as they want, as long as they have the funds. No credit is permitted. The dice are thrown and the prices of the units are adjusted (see chart). All investors can then buy and sell as many units as they want. The dice are then thrown again.

The winner is the investor with the most money.

If the price of a commodity reaches £0, all trading in the commodity is suspended.

Score on Dice	Rubber	Chocolate	Tin
2	-£5	-£20	-£90
3, 4, 5	-£5	-£20	-£40
6	£0	-£5	-£20
7	+£5	+£5	+£20
8	+£5	+£10	+£35
9, 10, 11	+£10	+£20	+£60
12	+£10	+£25	+£90

---

1 It's Your Business:

1. What are the current trends for salaries in
   a. the Stock Market
   b. the manufacturing sector
   c. the Civil Service
2. What are the current trends in the financial markets?
   Is buying shares an investment or a gamble?

---

2 Write.

Write a report of your game describing the trends.

103

UNIT 11: Headhunting

First conditional; 'when' plus 'will"; Vocabulary.

Willis Well, Terry, I think it is time we got down to the nitty gritty.
Walker OK.
Willis My client is an American bank which wants to build up its operations in the City of London. My job is to headhunt the best young talent in the City and to make them offers they can't refuse!
Walker Sounds interesting.
Willis If you join my client, you'll have a starting salary of £80,000 basic per year plus a bonus.
Walker How big is the bonus?
Willis It depends. If you bring in new business of up to £1 million, you'll get a bonus of 0.5% of the total. If you bring in more than £1 million, you'll get a bonus of 0.75%
Walker Sounds reasonable. What about my job title?
Willis When you start, you'll be a junior executive vice president.
Walker Junior! I don't like that. What about a car?
Willis When you start, you'll have a BMW. When you become a senior vice president, you'll get a Mercedes.
Walker Not bad. I'm certainly interested in the job.
Willis Well if you're interested, I'll make you a formal offer in writing.
Walker Fine. If you can get it to me before Friday, I'll look at it over the weekend. I'll give you an answer as soon as I can and certainly before Wednesday.

1 Answer these questions:

1. Willis is a headhunter. Who is he working for?
2. What salary does he offer Walker?
3. What bonus does he offer Walker?
4. What job does he offer Walker?
5. What car does he offer Walker?
6. What car does Walker have at present?
7. Does Walker accept the job?
8. How old is Walker?

2 Complete these sentences with part of the verb (*make*).

1. He .... about £50,000 a year.
2. She's .... some real improvements in their quality control.
3. We .... a profit last year for the first time in years.
4. He always sits on the fence. He can never .... a decision.
5. Can I .... the point that the mark will almost certainly go down.
6. We're in business to .... money, not friends!

Now underline the expressions which contain **make**.

LANGUAGE STUDY

The two speakers are talking about something they think is likely or certain to happen in the future. Underline all the sentences containing **when**, **as soon as** or **if**. Notice the tenses of the verbs.

3 Practise saying these paying attention to stress and intonation:

1. We'll start as soon as he arrives.
2. If everyone's ready, we'll begin.
3. They'll let us know when they need some more.
4. If she likes you, you'll get the best jobs.
5. If you buy these, you'll never regret it.
6. We'll talk about that later, if you don't mind.

In what situation do you think you might say each sentence?

Set One: First Conditional

EXAMPLE
If you join my client, you'll have a starting salary of £80,000.

1 Make sentences using 'if' and 'will' for these situations:

1. You have had a very good interview for a job. You want the job. What do you say to your husband/wife after the interview?

   ....

2. The salesman has a good product but it is a little too expensive. You are keen to buy it but you want a price reduction of 3%.

   ....

3. Terry wants to see you at 10.00. You are in another meeting until 10.15.

   ....

4. Frank has a problem with his spreadsheet. You can help him but you want him to help you with your report.

   ....

5. Gail wants your report by Friday. It's being photocopied now and the post takes two days.

   ....

2 Match up the two halves:

1. If you buy our product   a. he'll kill me.
2. If you don't take this opportunity b. I'll be able to get back.
3. If he takes you to the Ritz   c. you'll never regret it.
4. If we arrange a meeting for 3.00   d. you'll really enjoy it.
5. If my boss finds out   e. you'll always regret it.

Write your answers here:

1	2	3	4	5

3 Complete the dialogue using the correct part of one of these verbs; sometimes you will need a negative.

| meet | accept | give | do | provide | want | offer |
| insist | cost | go down | | come | want | need |

Manager If we .... you a car, we'll have to give one to all our other sales representatives. If we .... that, it .... a lot of money and our profits ....

Hilary I .... unless you .... me with a car. If you .... to break into the car components sector, you .... someone like me and someone like me .... a car.

Manager And if we .... you a higher salary?

Hilary No I .... on having a car. If you .... my demands on this, I .... another job offer.

4 Listening.

Listen to the conversation between Willis and Walker. Note the demands made by Walker.

1. ....

2. ....

3. ....

Does Willis give a positive or negative reaction?

5 Which prepositions could complete these sentences? Sometimes more than one is possible.

1. Many companies are looking for financial analysts. They are .... demand.
2. If you want a copy of BP's annual report, write to the company secretary. The reports are available free .... demand.
3. The list price is $3000 but you can find them .... offer for much less.
4. Tom Hopkinson's books are .... sale .... all good bookshops.
5. They talked .... the possibility of him joining the company.
6. They argued .... the fringe benefits.

107

Set Two: 'When' with 'Will'

EXAMPLE
When you start, you'll have a BMW.

1 Make sentences using *when* or *as soon as* and *will* for these situations:

1. Terry is going to fax you a report. He wants your comments as soon as possible. You have no urgent work this morning.

   ....

2. You are not happy in Marketing. Next month you are moving to Accounts.

   ....

3. The salesman is going to give you a written proposal for an excellent new software package. You must get approval from Head Office.

   ....

4. Frank is still having problems with his spreadsheet. You have a lot of work to do.

   ....

5. Bob is jealous of Adrian. He doesn't know yet that Adrian is his new boss.

   ....

6. You are phoning someone from outside your office. The details he needs are in your office. It's urgent. You both have fax machines.

   ....

2 When or If ?

1. .... you agree to buy 20,000, we'll give you a 5% discount.
2. .... you have any problems, I'll be in my office.
3. We'll shut down that machine, ... this shift ends.
4. We'll go over the details later, ... you don't mind.
5. I'll talk to you about it, ... the meetings finishes.
6. .... you want to take a break soon, we will.
7. .... the summer comes, demand will drop.
8. .... you like, we can discuss that tomorrow.

Say each of the sentences so that they sound and feel natural.

2 Reading.

Walker has received various job offers. Compare these two offers and decide which is better.

Mexico City Savings and Loan Corporation

Dear Mr. Walker,

Thank you so much for coming to see me on Thursday. We wish to offer you the job of Head of our new London office at a salary of £92,000 a year. As you know, this is a new office which you will have to set up and run. Your job is a key one. If you make a success of it, you will establish an international reputation for yourself as well as for the bank. We are sure you are the person for the job.

Yours sincerely

J. Alcala

J. Alcala
President

Tokyo and Shanghai Investment Bank

Dear Mr. Walker,

We would like to offer you a post as a senior executive vice president with our bank in the European department in Moorgate Street, London.

If you accept our offer, you will have the following terms and conditions:

Basic salary: £80 000 p.a
Performance bonus: up to £1 million   0.5%
                   over £1 million   0.7%
Fringe Benefits: Medical Insurance and the use of a BMW.

We hope you will accept this offer.

Yours truly,

A. Watanabe

A. Watanabe
President Europe

109

Set Three: Vocabulary

1 These adjectives can be used to describe people. Are they positive (P) or negative (N)?

Think of a person who is like each of the adjectives. Write their initials beside each adjective. Check any you don't know in your dictionary.

wise	....	stupid	....
intelligent	....	forward-looking	....
decisive	....	odd	....
bad-tempered	....	big-headed	....
keen	....	obstinate	....

"He's unorthodox for a managing director, but he gets on well with the workers."

2 Fill in each space with one word:

I decided to take .... his offer. I took .... the responsibility for the UK division in June, 1987. My predecessor claimed everything was fine but I wasn't taken .... I knew there were problems and I set .... solve them. We needed to break .... the European market so I decided to set .... a production unit in Germany. We also needed to build .... our market share in the UK. To do this, we needed to bring .... our price by at least 5% and our productivity had to go .... by 10%. I spoke to the union leaders and set .... the problems.

Underline all the two-word verbs you have completed.

110

Set Four: 'When'/'if' with 'will'

1 Complete these honestly about yourself:

1. If I get promoted, ...
   ....

2. When I retire, I ....
   ....

3. If I continue to work as hard as I am at the moment, I ....
   ....

4. When my children grow up, ...
   ....

5. If I get a good salary increase this year, ...
   ....

6. When I go home this evening, ...
   ....

PAIR WORK – STUDENT 1

You are Walker. You want to work for the bank but the terms and conditions could be better. Try to reach agreement with the bank but at the same time try to maximize your score. (The banker will also be trying to maximize his score!)

Salary

£80,000   score 1
£90,000   score 3
£100,000   score 5

Bonus

up to £1 million		0.5	score 1
		0.6	score 2
		0.7	score 3
over £1 million		0.7	score 1
		0.8	score 3
Job title		Senior Exec V.P.	score 2
Car		Mercedes	score 3

111

PAIR WORK – STUDENT 2

You are Ottenheim from the bank. You want Walker to work for you and you are prepared to negotiate some points. However, it is important that you don't concede too much or your other employees will become unhappy.

Try to reach agreement with Walker but at the same time try to maximize your score. (Walker will also be trying to maximize his score!)

Salary

£80,000	score 5
£90,000	score 3
£100,000	score 1

Bonus

up to £1 million	0.5	score 3
	0.6	score 2
	0.7	score 1
over £1 million	0.7	score 3
	0.8	score 1

Job title   Junior Exec V.P.   score 2

Car   BMW   score 3

1 It's your business.

1. Do you think the salaries available to International Bankers are excessive?
2. Do people talk about salaries in your company or are they a private matter? Is your salary satisfactory? When you get an increase, do you do anything to celebrate?

2 Write.

A press release saying that Walker has joined the bank.

Set Five: Using Real Texts

1 This text is difficult. Do not try to understand all of it. Which of these is the main message of the text?

a. You can't achieve all of your goals.
b. Goals can only be realistic and valuable if you revise them regularly.
c. Difficult goals can be your inspiration.
d. If you have a lot of goals, some of them will move into conflict with each other.

Making goals real

It's easy to achieve a goal. The toughest thing is to set realistic goals that you believe in and are inspired by, and then to monitor and update those goals frequently enough to keep them continuously powerful in your life.

It's amazing how many people drift away from the goal-setting technique after achieving some wonderful early results. Their first successes make them so busy that they stop growing. When that happens, they turn their backs on the most far-reaching technique for expanding their horizons and lifting their capabilities that humankind has ever devised.

To have goals that inspire you in the beginning, define them clearly. To have goals that are still inspiring in the middle of your drive for them, refine each one by adding exciting details as you learn more about them. To have goals that are inspiring all the way to the hour that you achieve them, take a moment every morning and night to vividly see yourself enjoying them.

Uninspiring goals are goals that you'll never stretch yourself to achieve. In other words, uninspiring goals are not strictly goals at all. To make your efforts pay back their full potential, keep your goals closely aligned with your latest thinking. That is, update your goals whenever you realize that you've taken another step towards a greater understanding of yourself.

You'll achieve many of your goals. Others you'll partially achieve. Still others you'll realize aren't worth paying the price for. Never hesitate to throw out a goal when you realize it isn't what you really want anymore.

(from **The Official Guide to Success** by Tom Hopkins)

How do you set your goals, and how often do you review them?

UNIT 12: Fringe Benefits

'Must' and 'have to'; Offers and suggestions; Financial Vocabulary

Graham Powell	Well, as you know, the company allocates a certain sum of money to be used for our employees benefit. This year we have to decide how to allocate £25,000 which is a 25% increase on last year. Of course, we don't have to allocate all the budget at the moment but I think we have to at least outline the general strategy. Shall we start with the suggestions from the union?
Union Rep	We feel we must do more for the retired workers. At present we give them an annual bonus at Christmas and then we do nothing for the rest of the year. We must do more.
Graham Powell	Yes, we must. And we'll have to do more for the children.
Union Rep	We don't have to. We give them a Christmas party and a summer camp. I think that is quite enough! We mustn't spend all the money on the kids!
Graham Powell	Perhaps you're right. Anyway, discuss this with your colleagues and then give me the union's view in writing.
Union Rep	OK. When do you want to meet again?
Graham Powell	We have to meet before the management meeting on the 17th so shall we say next Friday at 10.00?
Union Rep	OK.

1 Answer these questions, if you can:

1. What day is the meeting being held on?
2. How much money are they going to allocate? Is this the same as last year?
3. Does the Union Rep think they must spend more on the retired workers?
4. Does the Union Rep think they must spend more money on the children?
5. What is the Union rep going to do?
6. When is the next meeting?

LANGUAGE STUDY

Often the difference between **must** and **have to** is very small.
We use **have to** to talk about things which are necessary because of some objective necessity; for example, company policy or the law.
We use **must** or **'ll have to** to talk about things which are necessary because of a subjective necessity; the speaker thinks something is necessary.
Notice these two:
It is not necessary to .... = **You don't have to** ....
It is necessary not to .... = **You mustn't** ....
Underline the examples of all these verbs in the dialogue and decide why the speaker chooses that particular form.

2 Practise saying these, paying attention to stress and intonation:

1. You must let me know before Friday.
2. I have to finish this before the sales' conference.
3. You mustn't be late for the meeting.
4. I have the details on a handout so you don't have to take notes.
5. You don't have to come if you don't want to.
6. I'll have to do this at home on Sunday.
7. I'll have to come back to you on the exact details.
8. You don't have to travel Business Class, you know!

In what situation do you think you might say these?

STUDY TIP

To increase your confidence, practise important phrases by speaking very very quietly. Whispering is easier than speaking normally because you don't use your voice (it's also less embarrassing because nobody can hear you!). Concentrate on joining the words correctly. When you can whisper a phrase perfectly, you'll find it much easier to say it normally.

Set One: Necessity

1 Complete these sentences with either *must* or *have to*:

1. It's been nice meeting. We .... stay in touch.
2. We .... submit our VAT returns quarterly.
3. Next time you're in Milan, you .... come and see us.
4. Reception looks terrible. We .... give it a facelift.
5. Sorry, we .... wear protective glasses in this part of the factory – safety regulations, you know.
6. I'm sorry. All visitors .... sign in and wear badges.

2 Complete these sentences with either *mustn't* or *don't have to*.

1. If you don't like the canteen food, you .... eat there.
2. Come for a drink. You .... finish that report until next week.
3. You .... forget to bring the sales figures with you.
4. Italy is a good market. We .... miss this opportunity.
5. You .... bring your car. You can come with me.
6. We .... spend too much time on the details. Let's keep to the main point.

LANGUAGE STUDY

If something is generally necessary, use **(have) to**. When you suddenly see a particular thing is necessary, use **'ll have to**.

3 Use *(have) to* or *'ll have to* in these:

1. The lift isn't working again. We .... call the engineer.
2. If you want to start a business, you .... have capital and confidence.
3. We .... report weekly to the Sales Manager.
4. Sorry. The line is very bad. I .... ask you to spell that again.
5. This car is very unreliable. I .... ask for a new one.
6. With the amount of travelling I do, I .... have a reliable car.

4 Talk about your situation at work.

Think of things it is necessary for you, or your department to do. Think both of the general situation, and of what is happening at work at the moment. Use some of the language you have just practised.
You could talk about :

                Head Office   training courses   accounts
                tax   working hours   holidays

5 Listening.

Look at the union's suggestions for the allocation of the budget. Does it seem reasonable remembering that:

1. Inflation is at 10%.
2. The leader of the union likes fishing.
3. The Managing Director likes opera.

	last year	proposed
Pensioners' annual bonuses	3,000	3,500
Pensioners' trips	0	2,500
Children's party	2,000	2,500
Children's camp	6,000	6,500
Visits to Opera	2,000	1,000
Visits to Cinema	3,000	4,000
Fishing lake	4,000	5,000
TOTAL	**20,000**	**25,000**

Listen to Graham Powell and the Union Rep discussing the budget. What do they decide?

Pensioners' annual bonuses	....
Pensioners' trips	....
Children's party	....
Chidren's camp	....
Visits to Opera	....
Visits to Cinema	....
Fishing lake	....
TOTAL	25,000

6 Find five words which can fill each column in this diagram. Choose words which you think will be useful to you.

Verb	Adjective	
....	....	
....	....	*budget*
....	....	
....	....	
....	....	

Set Two: Shall

LANGUAGE STUDY

We can use **shall** when we want to make or ask for suggestions or when offering to do things: Shall we say next Friday?

1 Make or ask for suggestions using *shall*.

1. John wants a meeting. Suggest Tuesday morning.

2. John wants to meet for lunch. Ask him to suggest where.

3. You are in the restaurant. Suggest you have a drink to start with.

4. Suggest you pay the bill. (Who would you say this to?)

5. Suggest you get down to business.

6. Suggest you take a 10 minute break.

2 Match the offer/suggestion to the answer:

1. Shall I meet you at the airport?
2. Shall I get you a glass of water?
3. Shall we finish here?
4. Shall we deal with the non-controversial items first?
5. Who shall we invite to the launch?
6. What time shall we start?

a. These things usually start about six o'clock.
b. No, it's all right. I'll get a taxi.
c. Yes please. I get very thirsty when I make a presentation.
d. Could I ask just one more question?
e. Good idea. Leave the controversial items to last.
f. Only our biggest customers, I think.

Write your answers here:

1	2	3	4	5	6

3 Reading.

The Managing Director received this memo from Head Office. Read it and answer the questions.

To: All Subsidiaries
From: Schweitzer, Head Office

CONFIDENTIAL

This memo provides briefing notes about the situation at our Yonta River production unit. This information is confidential and its circulation has to be severely restricted. You must only tell those of your subordinates who need to know the details and you must impress upon them the need for secrecy. The details of this memo must not be communicated to the press or other media.

The Yonta River production unit was set up ten years ago in full agreement with the Yonta River and State authorities. We knew that there was a potential problem with the disposal of highly toxic waste. It was agreed that we had to bury this in sealed drums at a depth of 10 metres. We have done this for the last ten years.

Recent tests by the Yonta River Environment Office have shown vastly increased levels of chemical pollution in Lake Yonta. It appears that there has been leakage from our waste disposal pits into the river. It appears likely that the company will face a claim for damages running into several million dollars. Clearly the company will fight this action but, in the meantime, we must work on the assumption that we are going to lose the action. We may have to close the Yonta plant completely. We will certainly have to spend at least five million dollars. We will have to find ways of making substantial savings in our operations. Please examine your forward budget very carefully and look for ways of cutting costs.

Remember! This mustn't get into the newspapers!

Schweitzer

True, False or Don't Know?

1. Schweitzer is the boss of the company.
2. Everybody must read this memo.
3. It is all right to tell TV but not newspapers.
4. The Yonta River unit is new.
5. The factory is buried 10 metres below ground.
6. The chemical pollution comes from the toxic waste.
7. The company will have to close the Yonta plant.
8. It is certain to lose.
9. The MD will have to cut costs.
10. He will have to sell the fishing pool.

Set Three: Vocabulary

1 Which is better?

1. worth a lot   worthless   ....
2. highly priced   priceless   ....
3. work hard   hardly work   ....
4. small profit   profitless   ....
5. make a fortune   lose a fortune   ....
6. valuable   invaluable   ....
7. coherent   incoherent   ....
8. fortunate   unfortunate   ....

2 Match the words:

1. hourly   a. steward
2. skilled   b. paid
3. office   c. worker
4. shop   d. work
5. piece   e. payment
6. incentive   f. staff

Write your answers here:

1	2	3	4	5	6

3 Complete the following text using the words:

**profit   loss   shares   shareholders   borrow   overdraft
debentures   debenture   holders   loan   dividend**

There are different ways a company can have funds.

1. People can buy a part of the company. They are given certificates called .... The people are called .... If the company makes a .... they may receive money as a ....

2. People can lend money to the company and are paid a fixed rate of interest even if the company makes a .... They are given certificates called .... The people are called ....

3. The company can .... money from the bank. This can be a fixed sum for a fixed period, a bank ...., or the bank may give the company a facility to borrow money when it requires up to an agreed limit. This is called a bank ....

Set Four: Vocabulary

1 Find five verbs which can fill the column in this diagram. Choose words which you think will be useful to you.

Verb	
....	*money*
....	
....	£5,000
....	
....	

When we talk about **money**, we often use a word to talk about the quantity, for example **a lot of money**. How many quantity words can you think of which go in front of **money**. Write them here:

....

....

2 Find the verb and noun which best go together:

1. run
2. negotiate
3. borrow
4. own
5. owe
6. fund

a. money
b. money
c. growth
d. a company
e. a loan
f. shares

Write your answers here:

1	2	3	4	5	6

PAIR WORK – STUDENT 1

You are the Union Rep. Graham Powell wants to cut the budget (see page 117). You must try to protect the pensioners and the children. Your members like the cinema and you like fishing.

PAIR WORK – STUDENT 2

You are Graham Powell. You have agreed the proposed budget (see page 117) with the Union Rep. You have just received an order from your boss telling you to reduce the sum spent on employees to £15,000. Tell the Union Rep and decide on a new budget.

(Remember!! Your direct boss is a big fan of opera. You have 3 children.)

1 It's Your Business.

1. What fringe benefits does your company give its employees?
   Who allocates these?
   Which of these would you most like to have? Put them in order.

....	Travelling expenses
....	Subsidised meals
....	Subsidised travel
....	A company car
....	Interest-free loans
....	Reductions on your company's products

2. What budgets do you help prepare? How do you decide?

"Who put a middle-management chair at my top executive's desk?"

2 Writing.

Write a memo asking a colleague for a meeting. Suggest a time. Ask for an alternative if your suggestion is not suitable.

Set Five: Using Real Texts

1 This text is difficult. Do not try to understand all of it. Which of these is the main message of the text?

a. It's a good idea to complain about problems.
b. Trenell likes problems.
c. Describe your problem and what you want to happen in measurable, observable terms.

The First Secret : One Minute Goals (Part One)

When I got up there, he said, *Tell me, Trenell, what your problem is – but put it in behavioural terms.*
Behavioural terms? I echoed. *What do you mean by behavioural terms?*
I mean, the manager explained to me, *that I do not want to hear about only attitudes or feelings. Tell me what is happening in observable, measurable terms.*
I described the problem as best I could.
He said, *That's good, Trenell! Now tell me what you would like to be happening in behavioural terms.*
I don't know, I said.
Then don't waste my time, he snapped.
I just froze in amazement for a few seconds. I didn't know what to do. He mercifully broke the dead silence.
If you can't tell me what you'd like to be happening, he said, *you don't have a problem yet. You're just complaining. A problem exists only if there is a difference between what is* actually *happening and what you* desire *to be happening.*
Being a quick learner, I suddenly realized I knew what I wanted to be happening. After I told him, he asked me to talk about what may have caused the discrepancy between the actual and the desired.

(from **The One Minute Manager** by Kenneth Blanchard and Spencer Johnson)

(The conversation continues in Unit 13)

UNIT 13: White Widgets

Second Conditional; First and second conditionals; Vocabulary.

(on telephone)

Fenton Frankly, Mr Harris, you're wasting your time. We've bought our widgets from Universal Widget for the last fifteen years and we've always been very satisfied. If I were you, I'd try some other company.
Harris But what if I offered you a discount of 10%.
Fenton Well, of course, I'd be interested.
Harris And, if I gave you green or red for the same price as white?
Fenton Yes. That would certainly interest me. But before I come to any agreement, I need a lot more details.
Harris Well, if I came to see you on Tuesday, would that be convenient?
Fenton Not so fast, Mr Harris. Perhaps if you sent me some details on paper?
Harris Certainly. I'll send you our brochure and a copy of our standard agreement today......

1 Answer the questions:

1. Who supplies Mr Fenton with widgets at present?
2. How long have they been suppliers?
3. What company does Mr Harris work for?
4. What discount does Mr Harris offer?
5. What other advantages does he offer?
6. Is Mr Fenton interested?

2 Find five words which can fill each column in this diagram. Choose words which you think will be useful to you.

Verb	Adjective	
....	....	
....	....	*agreement*
....	....	
....	....	
....	....	

LANGUAGE STUDY

We use **if + past, would** when we are talking about things which might happen, but probably not. Underline examples of these in the dialogue. Why do you think Mr Harris uses **if + past, would** and not **if + present, will**?

3 Say the following, paying attention to stress and intonation:

1. I'd do it if I had the time.
2. If Frank read his spreadsheet manual, he wouldn't keep asking me for help.
3. If I came on Tuesday, would you have time to see me?
4. He'd like it if he saw it.
5. If I were 10 years younger, I'd leave this company.
6. If I knew, I'd tell you, but I'm afraid I don't know.

In what situation do you think you might say each sentence?

STUDY TIP

Many good language learners practise silently. Improve your English when you go to the supermarket by discussing what you want to buy in your head. Express what you really feel about your problems at work, but silently in English.

Set One: Second Conditional

EXAMPLE

If I offered you a discount of 10% that would certainly interest you.

1 Match up the parts of the sentence:

1. If I left every day at 5.00
2. If my secretary left me
3. If you were Prime Minister
4. If we lost that contract
5. If taxes were cut

a. people would work more.
b. I'd never get my work done.
c. I'd be completely lost.
d. I'd emigrate.
e. we'd be in big trouble.

Write your answers here:

1	2	3	4	5

2 Match up the parts of the sentence:

1. We'd save a lot of time
2. We'd lose at least a month
3. We'd spend less time waiting
4. We'd allocate more time at this meeting
5. We'd be more willing to invest the time

a. if we were sure of the long-term benefits.
b. if we had fixed appointments.
c. if we flew.
d. if we sent them by sea.
e. if we didn't have such a full agenda.

Write your answers here:

1	2	3	4	5

Notice many of the verbs which can be used to talk about money (**save, spend, invest**) can also be used to talk about time.

3 Complete these sentences in as many ways as possible:

1. I'd be happy if ....
2. I'd be unhappy if ....
3. My company would have big problems if ....
4. I'd lose my job if ....
5. I could stop work if ....

4 Listening.

Look at the current terms offered by Universal Widget. Then look at the terms proposed by Harris. If Fenton sees Harris, what comment do you think he will make? What will he ask for?

Current Terms from Universal Widget

Price

Widgets	White	£20
	Other Colours	£23
Superwidgets	White	£35
	Other Colours	£38

Discount
  3% for orders over 1,000 widgets.

Payment at 30 days.

1% per month interest charged after 30 days.

Current Terms from Harris Widget

Price

Widgets	White	£22
	Other Colours	£22
Superwidgets	White	£38
	Other Colours	£38

Discount
  Negotiable

Payment at 60 days

Interest may be charged after 60 days.

Listen to the meeting between Mr Fenton and Mr Harris. What terms do they agree?

....

....

Set Two: First/Second Conditional

1 Decide if the speaker thinks the following are likely (L) or not very likely (X):

1. If there was another crisis on Wall Street, I'd still be OK.
2. If the yen is devalued, it'll help our profitability.
3. If our company goes bankrupt, I'll retire.
4. If I got an increase in salary, I'd change my car.
5. It'd be a miracle, if I was promoted.
6. If they took my car from me, I wouldn't get another.
7. If they take my car from me, I'll get another straightaway.
8. I'd jump at it, if they offered me a job in the States.

2 Complete the sentences using one of these verbs:

1. If they give me a Golf, I ....   (stay)
2. If they gave me a Mercedes, I .... a ten year contract!   (sign)
3. If the dollar falls, we .... a good profit.   (make)
4. If the dollar fell by 20%, we .... millionaires.   (become)
5. If you meet your target, you .... a bonus.   (get)
6. If you doubled your target, you .... my job!   (get)
7. If you believe that, you .... anything   (believe)
8. If I were you, I .... a word he says.   (not believe)
9. If the factory closes, men over 50 .... new jobs in this area. (not get)
10. If they were prepared to move to London, they .... new jobs with no difficulty. (get)

LANGUAGE STUDY

Remember you can always make a condition stronger by using **providing** instead of **if**, for example:

You'll get a bonus, providing you meet your sales target.
We'd have no difficulty getting on the early flight, providing we booked straightaway.

3   Reading.

Mr Harris found this article in a business magazine whilst he was waiting to talk to Mr Fenton.

Honesty is the best policy?

1. You discover that a colleague is stealing money from the company. Would you:

a. Advise him quietly to pay it back.
b. Send an anonymous note to the boss.
c. Tell the boss and take the credit.
d. Do nothing.

2. You visit a colleague's house socially. You notice a typewriter and various small objects taken from work. Would you:

a. Immediately ask him about them and advise him to take them back.
b. Talk to him at work the next day.
c. Tell his boss.
d. Do nothing.

3. You have a new boss. On his/her desk is a photo of someone you recognise as a close friend of yours from some years ago. Would you:

a. Tell your boss immediately.
b. Say nothing but look forward to meeting your old friend again in due course.
c. Wait until you meet your old friend at a social occasion, then tell your boss with suitable surprise.
d. Avoid all social occasions.

4. One night leaving work late, tired and hungry, you accidentally bump your car into the Chairman's Rolls. There are no witnesses. Would you:

a. Tell nobody.
b. Leave a note on the Rolls accepting full responsibility.
c. Decide he deserved it and feel pleased.
d. Send a note to the Chairman describing another car which you say you saw bump his.

Unfortunately the rest of the questionnaire was missing. Add one more question and make up a scoring system for the test.

Try the test on a colleague. Use '**I think I'd probably** ....' to talk about these situations.

Set Three: Vocabulary

1 Find the opposites of these adjectives:

1. dangerous
2. permanent
3. hostile
4. interesting
5. expensive
6. gradual
7. lucky
8. horrible
9. daring

a. cheap
b. unlucky
c. timid
d. boring
e. friendly
f. wonderful
g. temporary
h. sudden
i. safe

Write your answers here:

1	2	3	4	5	6	7	8	9

2 Which of the words in exercise 1 can be used in front of:

a. a person
b. a product
c. a meeting

3 Complete, if possible:

Verb	Adjective	Person	Object
1. produce	productive	producer	production
2. manufacture	....	....	....
3. sell	....	....	....
4.	....	buyer	....
5. purchase	....	....	....
6.	....	exporter	....
7. import	....	....	....
8. manage	....	....	....
9.	....	director	....
10. supply	....	....	....
11.	....	....	advertising

Set Four: Vocabulary

1. Match the verbs to the nouns (more than one combination may be possible for each verb):

				Write your answers here:
1.	give	a.	a deal	1. ....
2.	reach	b.	an agreement	2. ....
3.	cut	c.	a discount	3. ....
4.	charge	d.	a price	4. ....
5.	offer	e.	a reduction	5. ....
6.	make	f.	interest	6. ....

Check with a good dictionary (or teacher) to find as many useful combinations as possible.

STUDY TIP

Don't only use your dictionary to find the meaning of words. It can also help you to find extra meanings for words you already know and which words combine with important words you need.

PAIR WORK – STUDENT 1

You represent Universal Widgets. It is possible that you are going to lose one of your biggest customers. Try to negotiate a new contract (and maximise your score).

Price

Widgets   White   £20 score 5   £16 score 1
                     Other Colours   £23 score 5   £19 score 1

Superwidgets   White   £35 score 5   £31 score 1
                     Other Colours   £38 score 5   £34 score 1

Discount

3% for orders over 1,000 widgets. score 2

Payment at 30 days.

1% per month interest charged   after 30 days score 5
                                 after 60 days score 3
                                 after 90 days score 1

PAIR WORK– STUDENT 2

You are Mr Fenton. The offer from Harris is quite good but you would prefer to continue working with Universal Widgets as you know their quality is excellent. Try to re-negotiate the terms to your advantage (and maximise your score).

Price

Widgets	White	£20 score	1	£16 score	5
	Other Colours	£23 score	1	£19 score	5
Superwidgets	White	£35 score	1	£31 score	5
	Other Colours	£38 score	1	£34 score	5

Discount

3% on all orders score 2

Payment at 30 days.

1% per month interest charged   after 30 days score 1
after 60 days score 3
after 90 days score 5

1 It's Your Business.

1. Does your company usually work with the same group of suppliers or does it put every contract out to tender?

2. What would your company do if it lost its biggest customer?

2 Write.

Write a memo setting out the terms of the agreement which you have just reached.

Set Five: Using Real Texts

1 This text is difficult. Do not try to understand all of it. Which of these is the main message of the text?

a. Find a solution which solves all the problems. Combine solutions if necessary.
b. Trenell cannot solve problems.
c. You need to combine solutions to solve problems.

> **The First Secret : One Minute Goals (Part Two)**
>
> After that the One Minute Manager said, *Well, what are you going to do about it?*
> *Well, I could do A,* I said.
> *If you did A, would what you want to happen, actually happen?* he asked.
> *No,* I said.
> *Then you have a very bad solution. What else could you do?* he asked.
> *I could do B,* I said.
> *But if you do B, will what you want to happen really happen?* he countered again.
> *No.* I realized.
> *Then, that's also a bad solution,* he said. *What else can you do?*
> I thought about it for a couple of minutes and said, *I could do C. But if I do C, what I want to happen won't happen, so that is a bad solution, isn't it?*
> *Right. You're starting to come around,* the manager then said, with a smile on his face. *Is there anything else you could do?* he asked.
> *Maybe I could combine some of these solutions,* I said.
> *That sounds worth trying,* he said.
> *In fact, if I do A this week, B next week, and C in two weeks, I'll have it solved. That's fantastic. Thanks so much. You solved my problem for me.*
> He got very annoyed. *I did not,* he interrupted, *you solved it yourself. I just asked you questions - questions you are able to ask yourself. Now get out of here and start solving your own problems on your time, not mine.*
> I knew what he had done, of course. He'd shown me how to solve problems so that I could do it on my own in the future.
> Then he stood, looked me straight in the eye and said, *You're good, Trenell. Remember that next time you have a problem.*
> I remember smiling as I left his office."

(from **The One Minute Manager** by Kenneth Blanchard and Spencer Johnson)

UNIT 14: The Trainee

Giving advice; Present simple and continuous; Vocabulary.

Tom Hello, Bill. You don't look very happy.
Bill I'm not. It's my boss. He's impossible. I think he resents me because I went to Cambridge and he left school at sixteen. I'm sure he thinks I'm trying to get his job. He never reads the reports I write. He sends me to represent him at the Production planning meeting but he doesn't tell me what to do when I am there. He's got no delegating skills so when he goes away for a few days he leaves no instructions so all the work has to wait until he comes back! If he wants us to work, he should tell us what to do while he's away. I get really annoyed about it all.
Tom If I were you, I'd talk to him about it.
Bill I'm afraid listening skills aren't his strong point, either.
Tom You should invite him out for a meal. Perhaps he'd listen then.
Bill That's a good idea but I'm not sure it'll work.
Tom Look, you're a management trainee. Why don't you speak to the Training Manager about it.
Bill Yes. I think I'll do that. Can I get you a drink?
Tom That's very kind of you. An orange juice, please. Remember, I don't drink alcohol.

1   True, False or Don't Know?

1. Bill likes his boss.
2. He thinks his boss is jealous of him.
3. His boss delegates well.
4. Bill understands what he has to do in his job.
5. Bill decides to invite his boss out to dinner.
6. Bill decides to see the Training Manager.
7. Bill and Tom have known each other for a long time.
8. Tom invites Bill to have a drink.

LANGUAGE STUDY

What is Tom doing in the dialogue? Underline the important examples.
Should expresses what the speaker thinks is necessary. It is weaker and more personal than **must** or **have to** and is often used to give opinions or advice.

2   Practise saying these paying attention to stress and intonation.

1. Why don't you speak to the boss?
2. Why don't you find a new job?
3. You should get a different supplier.
4. You should take a break.
5. You should take more exercise.
6. If I were you, I'd ask for help.
7. If I were you, I wouldn't worry about it.
8. If I were you, I'd tell them you don't want to do it.

Say each of these examples twice:
a. in a sympathetic way.
b. to show you are annoyed.

Remember how you say things is often as important as what you say.

STUDY TIP

It is not important to have a perfect accent. English is spoken by millions of people with hundreds of different accents. What is important is to have an accent which is consistent and easy for people to understand. Scots have Scottish accents, so there is no reason why Germans should not have German accents.

Set One: Giving Advice

EXAMPLES

Why don't you speak to the Training Manager about it?
You should invite him out for a meal.
If I were you I'd talk to him.

1 For each situation, give some advice:

1. "I'm always tired by three in the afternoon."
   ....
2. "I can never find time to work. The telephone rings all day."
   ....
3. "I have a very bad relationship with my direct boss."
   ....
4. "I've been doing the same job for 6 years. I want to change."
   ....
5. "Our computer keeps breaking down."
   ....
6. "I can't live on my salary."
   ....
7. "I'd like to start my own business but I need money and advice."
   ....
8. "The person who shares my office smokes very heavily."
   ....

2 Find five words which can fill each column in this diagram. Choose words which you think will be useful to you.

Verb	Adjective	
....	....	*skills*
....	....	
....	....	
....	....	
....	....	

STUDY TIP

We use the word **skills** to talk about learning English too. Which skills do you need most– reading, writing, listening, speaking?
From time to time you need to talk to your teacher about what is most useful to you. This will help you to avoid wasting time and make your learning more efficient.

3 Find the correct sequence for this conversation. Then listen to the original on the cassette.

Peter
1. It's my wife. She says I'm spending too much time at the office and that I'm neglecting her and the children.
2. Yes, but how?
3. That's a good idea. Thanks a lot. I'll talk to my boss this afternoon.
4. John, I've got a problem.
5. Probably. You see, I'm preparing next year's Budget and it's got to be finished by the end of the month.
6. What do you think I should do?
7. That's a good idea but I haven't got time at present.

John
a. Is that true?
b. Well, I think you should make the time. After all, your family is just as important as your job.
c. I see.
d. Why don't you take her out to dinner?
e. How about taking a couple of days off at the end of the month? You're tired and you need the break. Take the family away for a few days holiday.
f. What is it?

Write the correct sequence here:

| | | | | | | | | | | | | |

Underline the sentences where Peter asks for, or John gives, advice.

4 Listening.

This is Bill's job description.
– To prepare reports requested by the Marketing Manager.
– To liaise with Production. In particular, to represent Marketing as an observer at the weekly production planning meeting.
– To review specialist publications and to select important items to be read by the Marketing Manager.
– In the absence of the Marketing Manager, to run the Marketing Department (2 other assistants plus a secretary).

Listen to the telephone conversation between the Training Manager and the Marketing Manager. Make a list of Bill's principal faults in the opinion of the Marketing Manager.

....

....

Set Two: Revision

1 Only one sentence in each pair is possible. Cross out the impossible sentence.

1. a. We need to increase our exports.
   b. We're needing to increase our exports.
2. a. What does Jenny like?
   b. What is Jenny liking?
3. a. I don't want to go to this meeting.
   b. I'm not wanting to go to the meeting.
4. a. I make a market study.
   b. I'm making a market study.
5. a. Do you know France well?
   b. Are you knowing France well?

2 Put the correct form of the verb in each sentence:

1. (work)

a. He .... here for 10 years but he left six months ago.
b. He .... here for 10 years and he will probably stay another twenty years.

2. (buy)

a. We .... twenty of those in April.
b. We .... twenty of these so far and will probably buy five or six more.

3. (feel)

a. I .... very tired for the last few weeks. I need to take a week's holiday.
b. I .... tired at the beginning of June so I took a week's holiday.

4. (be)

a. He .... unhappy for several months.
b. He .... unhappy so I had a long talk with him and now everything is OK.

5. (phone)

a. I .... him yesterday. I was too busy.
b. I .... him yet. I haven't had time.

3 Reading.

Read the letter which Bill received from Brendan and answer the questions.

Dear Bill,

Thanks for your letter. Sorry it's taken so long for me to reply but I've been very busy.

Our Management Training course is very different from yours. You spend a year or so in different jobs: we change jobs every three months. You have lots of in-service training: we have very little but we are almost automatically sent for a one year MBA course after five years. I think our system is better in the long run. I've learnt a lot about different areas of the company; Production, Marketing, Sales, Personnel etc...... It has certainly helped me to make up my mind about where I want to specialise in the future. As you know, when we were at University, I was very interested in the Sales and Marketing areas. However, I've now decided that my skills lie in a completely different area; Personnel! I know that you will be surprised but it's true; I love dealing with personnel problems.

And so to your personal personnel problem! What can you do about your difficult boss? Well, I think you should do one of the following:

a) have a good heart-to-heart talk with him.
b) ask for a transfer.
c) change companies.

I think the third solution is the best of these. Do you want me to try and get you a job here?

Keep smiling,

Brendan
Brendan

True, False or Don't Know?

1. Bill changes jobs every three months. ....
2. Brendan is a Management Trainee. ....
3. Bill is going to do an MBA. ....
4. Brendan would prefer to work for Bill's company. ....
5. Brendan advises Bill to get a new job. ....
6. Brendan thinks Bill should smile more at his manager. ....

Set Three: Vocabulary

1   Think of someone who or something which is:

1. annual
2. available
3. capable
4. competitive
5. controversial
6. economical
7. essential
8. expensive
9. experienced
10. unethical

"Did I hear someone use the word 'unethical'?"

2   Who in your company is responsible for these things? Write their initials in each case.

1. mailings
2. cashflow
3. after-sales service
4. catalogues
5. budgets
6. good team spirit
7. deciding holiday dates
8. brand names
9. complaints
10. equipment

Set Four: Vocabulary

LANGUAGE STUDY

In English, the word **get** does not have very much meaning. But it is important because it joins with many different words to make important and useful word partnerships. Here are some examples:

He thinks I'm trying to get his job.
I get really annoyed about it all.
Can I get you a drink?

---

1 Use one of the words below and part of the verb *get*.

| coffee | through | back | involved | upset |
| there | rise | name | anywhere | approval |

Use each of these words once only.

1. I'll .... as soon as possible.
2. Sorry. I tried to ring you yesterday but I couldn't ....
3. I doubt if we'll .... before ten.
4. I didn't .... your ....
5. We don't want to .... in an argument about money.
6. Can I .... you some .... ?
7. We need to .... from the Accounts department.
8. Please, don't .... I think you misunderstood what I meant.
9. They've just .... a .... of nearly 9%.
10. This discussion isn't ....

Underline the important word partnerships which include the word **get** in these examples.

11. If you check what I've written so far, I'll get on with the rest.
12. I'm really tired. I can't get down to anything.
13. We aren't going to enjoy this. Let's get it over with.
14. After the crisis, I needed a break to get away from it all.

PAIR WORK — STUDENT 1

You are the Training Manager. Look at the criticisms made by the Marketing Manager. (pg. 134). Think of advice you can give Bill to help him improve his job performance.

PAIR WORK — STUDENT 2

You are Bill, the Marketing Assistant. Look again at the opening dialogue (Pg. 134) and at the job description (page 137). Discuss your problems with the Training Manager and listen to his advice. Be prepared to argue.

1 It's Your Business.

Have you ever had this type of problem? What did you do?

What sort of Management Training is best for young people?

Which of the following does your company provide?

Pre-service training courses.

On-the-job training.

In-service training courses.

Residential training courses.

Sandwich courses.

Opportunities to study for professional qualifications.

Grants to staff on study leave.

2 Write.

Prepare a memo from the Training Manager to the Marketing Manager about the meeting.

....

....

....

....

....

....

....

Set Five: Using Real Texts

1 **This text is difficult. Do not try to understand all of it. Which of these ideas does the author agree with?**

1. Don't wait more than seven days to call buyers in the "hot" section.
2. You must persuade people in the "medium" section that they need your product.
3. Don't waste time on people in the "cold" section.
4. Contact all your potential clients once a week.

The Client-Buyer file

Break this file into three sections.

a. Hot. These are the people who have the need, are qualified to buy, and are sincerely interested in making a decision soon.

When buyers are truly interested, they'll make a decision within seven days. Now that doesn't mean they'll purchase *your* product within seven days, but they'll purchase *a* product within seven days. A Champion tries to work with between three and five highly motivated buyers at all times. Some of you have a large stack of all your leads – and you call none of them.

b. Medium. The second division in your client-buyer file is for the people who are apparently qualified, have the need, but are not yet highly motivated.

Perhaps they're waiting for some future event to heat their medium needs up to a hot need. If you're working with a thirty-month cycle, a buyer is medium a year after purchase, and hot when his old item is two years and four months old.

c. Cold. In the third section of your client-buyer file, keep all the leads you get from any source that you don't immediately classify as hot or medium. These are the people who were just looking, who walked in, or called in from ads or signs, and seem to have a mild or future need for what you sell.
Keep in mind that few people call on ads, or come in when they see a store or sign, unless they have a definite interest in the product or service that's offered. The average salesperson is far too quick to dismiss lukewarm people as being unworthy of any effort at all.

(from **How to Master the Art of Selling** by Tom Hopkins)

The Client-Buyer file seems simple in theory; what are the reasons why it is more difficult in practice?

UNIT 15: A Presentation

All language needed
for presentations.

Mellor Good evening. How do you feel when you give a presentation? Happy? Relaxed? Confident? Probably not.

Most people go through several days of worry before they give a major speech or presentation. But there really is no need to go through all that.

Would you be surprised to learn that anyone can give a good presentation just by putting into practice some simple techniques?

Is it possible that by listening carefully to what I say in the next thirty or forty minutes and by putting these ideas into practice you can become an effective speaker? Well the answer is 'Yes' and 'Yes'.

Anyone can make a good presentation just by following a few simple rules.

Rule One. Get people's attention. Everyone in this room is paying me full attention at this moment. How did I do it? I used what is called a 'hook'. At the start of every presentation, be it a one minute briefing to your boss or a one hour presentation to your shareholders, you need to find a 'hook' to get your attention. I'd like you to think back to my opening remarks. How did I 'hook' you?

1 True, False, or Don't Know?

1. Mellor is unhappy.
2. His audience is unhappy.
3. Anyone can give a good presentation.
4. Mellor knows the secrets of making good presentations.
5. You only need a 'hook' for long speeches.
6. Mellor used a 'hook'.

What exactly is a 'hook'?
Why is it important?
Mellor's hooks were all questions. Why, do you think?

LANGUAGE STUDY

When you start a presentation, you have to get your audience involved; 'hook' them. It is often a good idea to do this by asking questions; the questions you are going to answer in your presentation.
How does Mellor hook his audience?

2 Find five words which can fill each column in this diagram. Choose words which you think will be useful to you.

Verb	Adjective	
....	....	*point(s)*
....	....	
....	....	
....	....	
....	....	

3 What are these 'hooks' for? Practise saying them paying attention to stress and intonation.

1. Do you sincerely want to be rich?
2. How can Toxic Cleaning improve your life?
3. Why are so many people turning to Holder's Lager?
4. Who needs to double their income?
5. What ability do all great managers have?
6. Why do some people do more work in less time than you do?

Set One: Presentations

STUDY TIP
If you can make a good presentation in your own language, you can do the same in English. The language may be different but the way to prepare it should be the same.

1 Discuss.

Which of these things do you do if you have to make a presentation in English?

1. Write your speech in your own language and get someone to translate it. Yes/No
2. Write your speech in full in English. Yes/No
3. Write the principle ideas in English on cards. Yes/No
4. Practise the speech in your bath every night. Yes/No
5. Practise your speech in the room where you are going to speak. Yes/No
6. Don't practise your speech, so that it remains fresh. Yes/No
7. Check all your equipment, material, handouts and then check them again! Yes/No
8. Don't check them – it's the organiser's job. Yes/No
9. Assume your audience know very little about what you are going to talk about. Yes/No
10. Use visuals to help the audience to follow. Yes/No
11. Don't drink anything. Yes/No
12. Establish eye-contact with someone who looks friendly. Yes/No
13. Try to establish eye-contact with everybody. Yes/No
14. Turn your back on the audience. Yes/No
15. Put your hands in your pockets. Yes/No
16. Speak quietly. Yes/No
17. Speak quickly. Yes/No
18. Repeat important points more than once. Yes/No
19. Summarise everything at the end of your presentation. Yes/No
20. Make lots of jokes. Yes/No

Which points do you think are the most important?

What other points do you think are important?

Do you remember these points when you are making a presentation in English?

Spoken English is different from written English. A good piece of writing may not be very easy to understand if it is read aloud. Why?

2 Which of the following things would you be likely to find in a room where someone was going to do a professional presentation?

Slide projector	Overhead projector	Stapler
Flip-chart	Hole punch	Pencil sharpener
Pointer	Transparencies	Felt tip pen
White board	Board writer	Scissors
Notes	Handouts	Chart
Microphone	Board rubber	Paper clips

There is one place where you could find all the other things. Where?

What is the difference in these two sentences:

Could you look at the figure on page 2, please?
Could you look at the figures on page 2, please?

3 Listening.

Listen to the extract from a presentation. Check if these statements are true, if you can.

1. The franchising operation is doing well. ....
2. They franchise fast-food. ....
3. The franchise concerns only Europe. ....
4. Table one shows details of expenditure. ....
5. Income has increased by 5%. ....
6. All franchisees pay on time. ....
7. There are more franchisees in France. ....
8. Burton thinks the management team is good. ....

Look at question 6. What is the difference between **We arrived on time.** and **We arrived in time**.

4 Helping the audience.

Certain expressions are 'signposts' to indicate the different sections of your presentation. Which are used to begin a presentation (B), change topic (C), end the presentation (E)

1. If you can now look at table four, you will see ....
2. Next, ...
3. I want to begin by ....ing ....
4. In conclusion, ...
5. Finally, ...
6. First of all, ...
7. Moving on, ...
8. Could I have the next slide, please? ....

147

Set Two: Presentations

1. Find 'hooks' to begin the following presentations.

1. Your company
2. Your job
3. One of your company's products or services
4. A recent or proposed change in your company
5. Your home city (for visiting business colleagues)
6. (You decide)

2. Complete these sentences with phrases you could use in a presentation.

1. I'd like to begin by ....
2. I'd like to suggest that ....
3. I'd like to move on to ....
4. If you could turn to ....
5. If you could look at ....
6. Let's concentrate on ....
7. Let's examine ....
8. As you can see, ...
9. As you know, ...
10. As I have already explained, ...
11. Can I point out that ....
12. Can I emphasise that ....
13. Can I remind you that ....
14. Let's finish by ....
15. I'd like to end by ....

3 Reading.

When you make a presentation on television, you may not be communicating what you want to communicate. Market studies show that your audience will receive 50% of your 'message' from the way you dress, your hairstyle etc., 35% from your tone of voice and your body language and only 15% from what you say. Such ideas are not new. When John F. Kennedy was elected President of the United States, many experts said that he owed his narrow victory to Richard Nixon's poor showing on television. What did Nixon do wrong? He looked like he needed a shave! Nixon worked very hard on his television image with 'communications experts' and was rewarded with the Presidency. More recently, Margaret Thatcher is reported to have changed her hairstyle and lowered the tone of her voice on the advice of 'image consultants'. In the words of the old song, "It ain't what you say, it's the way that you say it".

The same principles apply for all speakers. You have to dress appropriately for your audience. You have to watch your body language, eliminating unnecessary 'ticks' and be sure that you are speaking clearly and audibly. The best way to do this is to film yourself with a video camera or get a friend to observe you practising. You know that you've got something important to say. Make sure that you get the message across.

Does the author agree with these statements?

1. It is more important to look good than to say something interesting. **Yes/No**
2. Nixon didn't speak as well as Kennedy. **Yes/No**
3. All politicians need to have 'communications advisors'. **Yes/No**
4. You must wear expensive clothes. **Yes/No**
5. You must walk around a lot. **Yes/No**
6. You need a video camera. **Yes/No**
7. Speak very quietly. **Yes/No**
8. Practise. **Yes/No**

Which of the statements do you agree with?

149

Set Three: Presentations

1 Discuss.

Audiences remember:

> 20% of what they hear

> 50% of what they see

> 80% of what they see and hear.

> What visual aids are useful in a presentation? What are their disadvantages?

> Adjust your presentation to include some visuals.

STUDY TIP

Your presentation will be most effective if you:

–keep your sentences short.

–repeat important points by introducing them, explaining them and summarising them. Many good presentations have very few important points. Too much unnecessary language does not improve the presentation. It might obscure the important points.

–stress important ideas, particularly figures and dates, by repeating them immediately with no unnecessary language:

We have seen a twenty-eight per cent increase, twenty-eight per cent – in the present year.

The Italian launch will be in May and Germany in the Autumn – Italy, May (short pause) Germany, Autumn.

Don't be afraid to use very simple English.

–use correct intonation: pitch your voice high at the beginning of a sentence; make it go up if you have not finished your idea and for especially interesting words; and down at the end of your idea.

2 Make your own presentation.

Many business people need to make presentations of different kinds – their company, a product, the factory etc. To practise the essential language of presentations, you are going to give a short presentation.

a. Choose a topic you may have to give a presentation on yourself (think again of the hooks on page 144/5).
b. What can you include in the time? How many important points? How will you emphasise them?
c. Who is the presentation for? How much do they already know? What will they expect you to talk about?
d. Do you need 'extra' bits? To welcome people? To thank people? To introduce yourself?
e. What is the purpose of the presentation? What reaction do you want? What will make you think it is successful?

STUDY TIP

Good presentations follow the ABC pattern.

A. Tell them what you are going to tell them.

What is your hook? State your objective.

B. Tell them.

Develop your ideas. Give details.

C. Tell them what you've told them.

Summarise, repeat important ideas, conclude.

3 Discuss:

Audience attention almost always decreases in the middle of a presentation (the 'B' phase). What can you do to keep the attention? Adjust your presentation to take account of this.

4 Review this unit and then make your presentation to the rest of your class.

Listening Texts

Unit 1

Operator	Canton Computers. Can I help you?
Mr Powell	Could I have extension 577, please?
Operator	One moment, please. Putting you through.
Man	Maintenance Department.
Mr Powell	Mr Davis?
Man	Sorry? Who do you want?
Mr Powell	Davis, John Davis.
Man	Well, there is no Davis here. Hold the line and I'll put you back to the switchboard. (wait)
Operator	Who did you want, sir?
Mr Powell	Davis. John Davis
Operator	I'm sorry. We have no-one of that name working in the company.
Mr Powell	Oh forget it. (slams down phone)

Unit 2

Phil	Can you spare me a few minutes, Tim? We've got a problem with John David's expenses.
Tim	Not again. What has he done this time?
Phil	Well he went to a meeting in France and this morning he put in a bill for £820.
Tim	820 quid for one meeting. You must be joking.
Phil	See for yourself.
Tim	Goodness. Let me see. I suppose that you have checked the cost of the plane?
Phil	Yes. That seems correct.
Tim	I thought hotels in France were cheap by our standards.
Phil	Yes, it seems excessive. It shouldn't really come to more than £50 a night, say £60 in Paris.
Tim	The dinner seems reasonable
Phil	No. That's a lot for Paris. You can eat well for £20. Probably less than that in Lyon.
Tim	What about the dinner with the agent?
Phil	They must have gone to one of the 3 star restaurants. Even so £130 seems a lot. Still, he has given us the bill. And as for that miscellaneous £60, it was probably half that.
Tim	OK. I'd better see Mr David. Why do people always try to fiddle their expenses?

Unit 3

Operator	Switchboard
Stepniewski	Could you help me please? I want to put through a call to Sweden. Can I dial direct or do you have to get it for me?
Operator	You can dial it yourself, madam. Dial 9 and you will get an outside line.
Stepniewski	Could you give me the code for Sweden, please?
Operator	Yes certainly. You dial 01046 and then the number you want.
Stepniewski	Sorry, that was too fast for me! Could you repeat the code, please? And would you mind speaking a little more slowly?
Operator	Terribly sorry, madam. 0..1..0..4..6 .
Stepniewski	01046, thank you. And how much does it cost?
Operator	Well it varies according to the time of day. If you call now, it will cost about 75p a minute but it's much more expensive during the day: £1.20 between 8am and 1pm and £1 between 1pm and 9pm.
Stepniewski	Thanks. Could you give me a morning call, please?
Operator	Certainly. Would you mind giving me your room number, please?
Stepniewski	Room 506.
Operator	What time would you like your call?
Stepniewski	Quarter to seven, please.
Operator	Six forty-five. Do you want a cup of tea or coffee and a newspaper?
Stepniewski	Coffee and the Times, please.
Operator	Thank you, madam.
Stepniewski	Thanks.

Unit 4

Hutton	Freddy Hutton speaking.
Abbotts	Hello, Freddy. This is Brian. How are things?
Hutton	Not so bad, Brian. We've caught up quite well with the backlog.
Abbotts	Can you give me the figures for the end of week 15?
Hutton	Sure. We've sent 20,000 AB122s, 16,000 AB132s, 5,000 AD122s, 10,000 GK122s, 3,000 JK112s and 40,000 YZ113s.
Abbotts	Sixteen thousand AB132s and 5000 AD122s.
Hutton	That's right.
Abbotts	And sorry, did you say YZ113 or YZ130?
Hutton	1 - 1 - 3.
Abbotts	So you haven't sent any GJ 134s or YZ 130s yet?
Hutton	Not for the moment.

Abbotts	If my calculations are exact you still have to send 4,000 AB132s, 15,000 AD122s, 15,000 GJ134s, 10,000 GK122s, 17,000 JK112s and 40,000 YZ130s. Do you agree with that?
Hutton	Yes.
Abbotts	Good luck with the production then.

Unit 5

Phil	Well, Mr Baxter, I'm afraid that my report on your department is not going to be very good.
Baxter	Not good? Why?
Phil	Well I noted two main problems. The first is with absenteeism, particularly in your accounts receivable section. You have 8 people in the department but you rarely have all 8. You usually have one or two absent and there are sometimes 5 people away!
Baxter	Yes, well there is at the moment, I admit. But that's because it's winter. Most of the women in receivables have got children. And in winter, the children get ill and the mothers have to stay at home and look after them. You can't expect the fathers to take time off, can you?
Phil	Why not? Your attitude seems very sexist to me! Anyway the result is that a lot of customers owe you a lot of money.
Baxter	OK, perhaps that's true but it certainly isn't true for the Accounts Payable section. We are well on top of the work there.
Phil	Exactly. That's the second problem. You are too efficient! You pay bills before you need to! Your department is not very good at getting money in but good at sending it out.
Baxter	Our suppliers expect to be paid on time. If we don't give them good service, they'll give us bad service. I don't want the factory to stop because we haven't paid some small bills.

Unit 6

Thomas	Could you tell me a bit more about this exhibition? I understand that you're going to have a nightly TV show from it.
Dewan	That's right. As you know, we are part of the same group as Galaxy TV. They're producing a 30 minute programme every evening featuring some of the products from the Show. This is going out from 9.30 to 10.00 every evening on the News Channel. Of course, we're mainly going to feature the new computers and so on but we're also going to feature more specialist products, such as your Power Protector.
Thomas	Who's presenting the programme?

Dewan	Jean Cooper. She's just joined us from the BBC. This is going to be her first programme for us.
Thomas	That sounds very interesting. Now could you give me a few more details of the costs? I've read your brochure but some things are not very clear.(tape fades)

Unit 7

Newsreader	Contrasting economic news today from 2 EC Countries. Here is Cathy Connolly with the details.
Connolly	The two countries are Germany and Italy. Germany has announced a record trade surplus. Exports have increased by 20% this year whilst imports have gone up by only 5%. Experts confidently predict that the mark will be revalued within the EMS in the next couple of days. This will be good news for British companies who will find it easier to sell their products in the highly lucrative German market. Different news from Italy where inflation is currently at 10%. The Italian government today announced an increase of 3% in interest rates and a devaluation of 5% in the lira. This is likely to have an immediate deflationary effect on the Italian economy. It also makes holidays in Italy even more attractive.

Unit 8

Freddy	Harry? You know those new silicon widgets they were talking about in the trade press? I've put in an order for 1000 on a trial basis. Can you test them out?
Harry	Sorry, Freddy. I've got a lot of work on at the moment. I won't be able to test them for at least a month.
Freddy	Look, I don't often ask you a favour, do I?
Harry	I suppose not.
Freddy	And they've certainly had good write-ups in the trade press, haven't they?
Harry	Well, yes, they have.
Freddy	So it's in everybody's interests to test them quickly, isn't it?
Harry	Yes, you're right. I'll test them as soon as they arrive.
Freddy	Great. They're coming on Tuesday.
Harry	Well, I'll give you an answer by Friday.
Freddy	Thanks.

Unit 9

Secretary	Mrs Tait's secretary.
Agent	This is Brooklyn Travel. I'm returning your call about Mrs Tait's trip to the South of France.
Secretary	Oh yes.
Agent	Well there are planes to Nice leaving at seven thirty and at ten but I'm afraid they're both fully booked for the morning of the eighth. It's possible to get a place on the one at twelve fifteen or else Mrs Tait could catch the evening plane on the seventh.
Secretary	She's got an appointment on the afternoon of the seventh. What time is the last flight?
Agent	At eight twenty, arriving in Nice at eleven o'clock local time. We could book her a room in a hotel near Nice airport and she could collect her car on the morning of the eighth.
Secretary	That's certainly possible. You said there was a place on the eleven fifteen flight on the eighth.
Agent	Not eleven fifteen, twelve fifteen. The problem is that it won't arrive in Nice until nearly three o'clock local time. By the time she has got through customs, got her car and driven to Sophia Antipolis, it'll be about five o'clock.
Secretary	That's too late. Book her a place on the evening flight on the seventh plus a hotel at the airport.
Agent	Fine. As for the car, a Peugeot 205 will be OK, won't it?
Secretary	Did you say 205 or 405?
Agent	205.
Secretary	Good. Mrs Tait likes small fast cars.

Unit 10

In 1970, the dotte was strong and stood at 7 dollars to the dotte. Over the next ten years, there was a gradual fall in the value of the dotte until in 1980 it stood at 5 dollars. In 1981, it fell sharply to 3 dollars.

In 1982, it rose to 4 dollars but then it dropped by 1 dollar in 1983.

It dropped to 2 dollars in 1984 and levelled off until 1986 when it went up by 3 dollars.

In 1987 it increased to 6 dollars and reached a peak of 8 dollars in 1988 before decreasing to 7 dollars in 1989. It remained at 7 dollars throughout 1990.

One year ago, our average weekly production was about 50,000 units. In fact the figure for week 1 of this year was 49,500.

In week 2, we introduced our new piece-rate system. This had an immediate effect on production. In week 2, our output was 61,000. During the period week 3 to week 8, we produced about 60,000 units per week.

In week 9, we had a three day strike and production fell to 28,000 units but this figure rose by 30,000 in the following week. Over the next 20 weeks, we continued to produce about 58,000 units per week.

We shut down completely for the next three weeks, the factory holidays. We produced nothing during weeks 31 to 33 but this gave us a chance to do some essential maintenance work. As a result, production went up.

Week 34, the first week after the holidays, was poor: we only produced 48,000 units. However, in week 35 we achieved an output of 63,000 units.

We are now in week 49. Average weekly output has been at 63,000 since week 35. We think production will remain at this level for the rest of the year.

Unit 11

Willis   You've had time to consider the offer, Terry. What do you think?
Walker   I'm not too sure, David. To be honest I've had another offer from a Japanese bank which wants to develop in London. I'm not so sure that the offer from your client is such a good one. I'm not completely against it but it'll cost you. You see, people in my job are in demand right now. If I tell my present employers that I'm thinking of leaving, they'll probably offer me a large increase.
Willis   So what more do you want?
Walker   Well, I'm not too happy with the job title. I think I should be a senior exec not a junior. And then a Mercedes is a much better car than a BMW, isn't it? And the salary could be better. I'd like to work for your client but ....
Willis   But these things can always be negotiated, Terry. If you talk to Paul Ottenheim, you'll be able to reach a satisfactory compromise. When you talk to him about the job and the prospects, you'll really want to do it.
Walker   Will I, David? Will I?

Unit 12

Powell	I've looked at what you've suggested and I broadly agree with your proposals.
Union Rep	Good
Powell	With one big exception. Opera.
Union Rep	Opera is an elitist concept. It is not for the workers. Managers should pay for their special interests out of their own pockets.
Powell	What about the fishing? How many of your members go fishing?
Union Rep	More than go to the opera anyway.
Powell	Look. We must come to a compromise. Can we agree that the fishing budget goes up to 5000 but that the Opera goes up to 2500?
Union Rep	OK but where do we take the 1500 from?
Powell	Shall we take a few hundred off each of the cinema and the pensioners' trips?
Union Rep	500 off the pensioners!
Powell	OK. And a thousand off the cinema.
Union Rep	We agree. You've got a deal.

Unit 13

Harris	As you can see Mr Fenton these are excellent widgets.
Fenton	Yes they are but they are expensive. At least the white ones are. If you want to do business with us, you'll have to reduce those prices.
Harris	Well if you ordered more than a thousand, we would happily consider a discount.
Fenton	And if I gave you a trial order of 300, would you give me a discount?
Harris	Yes
Fenton	How much?
Harris	3%
Fenton	OK You've got a deal for 300 green widgets.

Unit 14

Training Manager	Hello, Malcolm. This is Derek. I'm ringing about your assistant Bill Hurley.
Marketing Manager	Uh huh
Training Manager	It's time for his annual interview. What do you think of his performance?

Marketing Manager	Not a lot really. I don't think he's very good. He just doesn't have the necessary skills. Knowledge but no skills, that's him.
Training Manager	Why do you say that? Surely it's not as bad as that.
Marketing Manager	It is. He's supposed to prepare me reports. I want one or two pages setting out the principal ideas. He prepares 50 pages and doesn't even reach a conclusion.
Training Manager	What about his contact with the Production department?
Marketing Manager	They hate him. He spends all his time telling them how to organize their production better. I've told him to speak less and listen more but he continues just the same.
Training Manager	Anything else?
Marketing Manager	He's supposed to simplify my life by reading the trade press and finding articles of interest for me to read. He finds so many that I'm doing more reading, not less. And as for leaving him in charge of the office...the last time he made my secretary cry and upset everybody else. He's got no inter-personal skills at all.
Training Manager	Can you think of no good points?
Marketing Manager	No. A Business School education might train you to be a good Managing Director but it certainly doesn't make you a good marketing assistant.

Unit 15

Burton	What has gone wrong? Why have we got into such financial difficulty? First of all, if you can look at table one, you will see a breakdown of our income for the last twelve months. You will notice that income has fallen by 5% compared with the previous year. What has caused this? Well, essentially there are two factors; the reduction of income from our franchisees in the Far East and the high level of bad debts from franchisees. If you can now look at table two, you will see that our expenditure has continued to rise sharply. This is probably due to the large increase in the number of franchisees, particularly in France. However, if you refer back to table one, you will notice that we received virtually no income from these new French franchisees. In short, they cost us a lot but paid very little! My conclusion is that this whole operation has been very badly handled.